Welcome to Thebes

Moira Buffini's plays include *Blavatsky's Tower* (Machine Room), *Gabriel* (Soho Theatre), *Silence* (Birmingham Rep), *Loveplay* (Royal Shakespeare Company), *Dinner* (National Theatre and West End), *Dying for It*, adapted from *The Suicide* by Nikolai Erdman (Almeida), *A Vampire Story* (NT Connections) and *Marianne Dreams* (Almeida Theatre). She lives in London with her husband and children.

MOIRA BUFFINI

Welcome to Thebes

faber and faber

First published in 2010
by Faber and Faber Limited
74–77 Great Russell Street
London WC1B 3DA

Typeset by Country Setting, Kingsdown, Kent CT14 8ES
Printed in England by CPI Bookmarque, Croydon, Surrey

A CIP record for this book
is available from the British Library

ISBN 978–0–571–25873–4

2 4 6 8 10 9 7 5 3 1

To Mihret Tekie

on her journey throughout the time of writing

Welcome to Thebes was first performed in the Olivier auditorium of the National Theatre, London, on 15 June 2010. The cast was as follows:

THEBANS

Megaera Madeline Appiah
Sergeant Miletus Michael Wildman
Junior Lieutenant Scud Omar Brown *or* René Gray

Eurydice Nikki Amuka-Bird

Prince Tydeus Chuk Iwuji
Pargeia Rakie Ayola

Haemon Simon Manyonda
Antigone Vinette Robinson
Ismene Tracy Ifeachor

Tiresias Bruce Myers
Harmonia Alexia Khadime
Polykleitos Daniel Poyser

Aglaea Aicha Kossoko
Thalia Joy Richardson
Euphrosyne Pamela Nomvete

Eunomia Zara Tempest-Walters
Bia Karlina Grace
Helia Clare Perkins
Eris Irma Inniss
Xenophanes Cornelius Macarthy

Author's Note

I've been asked to write an author's note
To explain why I don't put all the full stops in.
The text is not poetry
It is drama
It needs to be useful to actors
And I think this is.

Characters

Megaera
a soldier

Sergeant Miletus

Junior Lieutenant Scudor

Eurydice
President of Thebes

Prince Tydeus
Leader of the Opposition

Pargeia
a senator

Haemon
Eurydice's son

Antigone
her niece

Ismene
her niece

Tiresias
a seer

Harmonia
his guide

Polykleitos
a mechanic

Aglaea
Foreign Secretary

Thalia
Minister of Justice

Euphrosyne
Minister of Finance

Eunomia
a student of law

Bia
Minister of Trade and Industry

Helia
Minister of Agriculture

Eris
Chief of Police

Xenophanes
Minister of Education

Theseus
First Citizen of Athens

Phaeax
his aide

Talthybia
a diplomat

Enyalius
Head of Athenian Security

Plautus
Athenian Security

Ichnaea
Athenian Secret Service

Aides, bodyguards, attendants, soldiers, citizens

WELCOME TO THEBES

A city named Thebes,
somewhere in the twenty-first century.

Prologue

Three Theban soldiers enter: Megaera, a woman of twenty, Miletus a sergeant of maybe thirty, Junior Lieutenant Scud, a boy of thirteen. It is dawn.

Megaera OK shut up

Miletus Anyone still talking now shut up

Scud SILENCE

Megaera Nobody make any sudden moves, nobody get up

Miletus Stay in your seats

Scud PHONES

Miletus Phones – any fucking disco tunes and I will not answer for my men

Scud You check them NOW

Megaera Put the booklets down. Don't read that shit

Scud All of you make sure those fuckers don't go off

Miletus Listen to the Junior Lieutenant – he don't like mobile phones

Scud They have bad energy and they affect your brain. I'm telling you for your own good

Megaera Anyone who wants the toilet I don't care. You missed your chance

Scud You've got to look for bomblets

Miletus I am insulted if the truth be known

Scud Get looking

Miletus Our orders are to search for unexploded submunitions. No equipment. For our mine detector we have got the Junior Lieutenant here

Scud They are called bomblets – and they're yellow.
Look like little cans of fizz
And children pull on them because their thirst is bad
BOOM
And you become a rain of meat
And women pulling bits of you from out their hair
And screaming oh disgusting get me some shampoo

Miletus What are you doing?

Megaera I'm sitting down here on my arse

Miletus Why?

Megaera I haven't finished with these people

Miletus What d'you want with them?

Scud jumps on some rubble.

Scud BOOM

Megaera To welcome them to Thebes

Miletus Don't tell them all your shit

Megaera Why not?

Miletus They'll leave

Megaera Are you the expert?

Miletus I would leave

Megaera I'm going to tell them Theban politics

Miletus No one understands that

Scud jumps on another pile of rubble.

Scud BOOM

Miletus Easy, son
Be easy
You stay right by my side

Miletus moves away, with Scud. Megaera holds up her gun.

Megaera The only politics in Thebes is this.
This has been the government for years.
I don't know how it started; I don't care
Some brother fighting brother for the power.
My politics began the day the soldiers came.
This is my shit and if you're scared to hear it
Close your eyes.
We heard their guns and ran.
I could feel bullets whooshing past my face.
I saw a man turn round and try to stop one with his
hand
Because he thought 'what's this?'
As if the bullet was a fly.
Whoosh
They trapped us by the river.
If I could describe you how it felt
They way they held me down and tore
You would be sick I know you would
Or scream and we'd be here all day
While you had counselling and cried.
After five or six I was unconscious I suppose.
The soldiers must have thought that I was dead
Because when I came to, I found myself
In a pile of bodies. My mother
And my sisters seethed with ants.
This is your introduction to our state
'Cause everybody has a tale like this.
I slipped into the river, floated to the fields
Time was not even. It was odd
It bends and it's misshapen in my mind

A day was like a month, a month a year
I don't think that I spoke one word.
I ate forest nuts and beetles, poor old me
My monthly bleeding never came again

Scud BOOM

Megaera And then Miletus found me
He's the sergeant there, my brother now.
He put this gun into my hand and
Made me human once again.
When we fall upon our enemies –
Always the men who did that to me –
Feelings come on me like I don't know
I am not scared of anything
No pain about my family
No cares
I am all powerful, all fire
I am revenge, Megaera; I am fury
Whoosh.
The furies have no laws other than their own
Which even Zeus himself has to obey.
These are my laws now
And this, my life of politics.
Peace?
Never, not for me

Miletus Megaera

Scud Dead bloke

*Miletus and Scud have discovered a corpse. Megaera
approaches.*

Miletus Look at that uniform
New boots, the golden braid

Scud spins, startled. He raises his rifle.

Scud Felt fingers down my back

Megaera Well, they ain't his
   He's maggot food

Miletus This is Polynices

Megaera How do you know?

Miletus His necklace

Megaera Fuck

Miletus General Polynices

Scud Did we fight for him?

Miletus No. He's the one who pulled you out of school,
his men –

   Scud reacts to this, the memory like a cuff.

When I picked you up I was with Creon's men, remember?
We fought for him till the stupid fucker got dismembered.
Then for Adrastus till he set himself on fire. Then we were
in the forest fighting everyone. Last we joined Eteocles.
He's the one who still had food

Scud Who do we fight for now?

Megaera That is the question, Scud

Scud I fought for you

Miletus I know

Scud The ghosts are grey

Miletus Come on

   Miletus leaves with Scud.

Megaera Welcome
   Welcome to Thebes

Act One

SCENE ONE

Enter Tiresias led by a Harmonia, a girl.
Enter Polykleitos, a mechanic. He sits amid a pile of rifle parts, dismantling weapons.
Enter Antigone, barefoot, objectless, alone.
The sound of a helicopter approaching from afar.

Enter Thebans and Athenians, preparing for a state event.
Antigone watches them as if their actions make no sense.

Talthybia runs on, an Athenian aide. Bottled water, paperwork, bad choice of footwear.
Harmonia is begging. Talthybia declines to give her a coin and exits hurriedly.

Harmonia approaches Antigone.

Antigone I have nothing
  Nothing no

Tiresias You have not survived this war
  You're breathing but you're not alive

Antigone Don't speak to me, Tiresias

Antigone begins to walk away. His voice arrests her.

Tiresias The dead see everything you do
  In darkness they have eyes that never close
  Up here, everyone is blind
  Think hard where you belong

She turns to him, pained.

You and your sister
  Last remnants of a cursed house
  Follow your destiny, Antigone

8

Antigone exits. The helicopter, louder.

Talthybia enters. A makeshift Theban choir begin to sing a national anthem.

   Other Athenian men and women enter in silk and linen suits, Theban officials in cheaper suits or trying to hold together their national dress in the face of the helicopter's gale.

The helicopter becomes deafening. One of the choir runs. Harmonia seeks cover.

   Tiresias remains, the only still point in the scene.

Helicopters are obviously beasts of terror in Thebes, for the makeshift choir has fled.

   Talthybia loses her hair-do. Everyone crouches in the blast.

The blast dies down. Talthybia rushes off, followed by soldiers and aides.

   Bodyguards and aides cross with all the luggage and paraphernalia of a diplomatic stay.

   Harmonia stands up, trying to see.

Theseus enters, a confident man in his prime. Talthybia is at his side.

Theseus Thebes

Talthybia We have our people working on a new hotel and embassy but at the moment there's two options, sir: the compound where our military are, or there's an invitation from the president elect, Eurydice, to stay here at the presidential palace. We've checked it over; basic but OK. A lot of art and artefacts; no electricity. There is no national grid right now

Theseus I'm staying here?

Talthybia It's a building of historic interest and much cooler than the compound. It also gets the breeze; built by Cadmus and Harmonia who founded Thebes

Theseus Do they have internet?

Talthybia At the compound we have internet

Theseus They got a phone?

Talthybia Mobiles, yes, amazingly. They seem to go on working even when the power is down

Theseus I want to call my wife

Talthybia I'm sure they're setting up a private line

Theseus Right now
  I feel like telling her I'm here

Talthybia Please borrow mine, sir. It would be such a privilege –

Theseus Sure

Talthybia To know that I've assisted with your communication

Phaeax joins them. Theseus dials.

Everyone has mobiles; it's astonishing. You go out to the villages and even in these little one-goat towns without a single flushing loo, everyone is talking on a mobile phone

Phaeax (*to Talthybia*) Excuse me, where's the band?

Talthybia Yes actually, there is no band

Theseus Hey, Phaedra – guess where I am
  Oh – could you get her?

Phaeax Theseus was told there'd be a band. He is expecting one

Talthybia Well very / sorry but

Phaeax If there wasn't one I should have been informed

Talthybia I did my best to get a band. The Thebans / told me this –

Phaeax He likes the music here

Talthybia The band are dead except the bass guitar
  He's alive but only one hand left

Theseus / She what?

Talthybia So then I tried to organise a choral group;
  Authentic local sound.

Theseus / OK

Talthybia But people don't like helicopters here. They've
gone

Phaeax Would you explain that to him, please?
  Because this is insulting
  I can't even see a fucking flag

  Phaeax exits.

Theseus Get her to call me on this number; thanks

Talthybia The city's still unstable, sir
  We didn't think it wise to make a lot of fuss

Theseus Quite so. I'd better keep this phone; she's going
to call me back

Talthybia That's absolutely
  What an honour
  Sir, I did intend for there to be some music as a welcome
but –

Theseus No commotion. Good

Talthybia I'm glad you think so

Theseus Yes. I've come here in humility
  I want to see first hand what we Athenians have done
  We've given common people here control of their own
fate
  The gift of democratic government

Talthybia The voting; frankly it was moving –

Theseus They need to see what democratic leadership can be

   Phaeax re-enters.

Phaeax Sir, they have some rooms prepared. Perhaps you'd like to freshen up? Before you meet the president elect

Theseus Just look at this old palace

Talthybia Soon to be renamed the congress

Theseus Dionysus – he was born here
  The great god Frenzy

Phaeax Yes sir

Theseus Bacchus
  Pulled from the thigh of Zeus
  Maybe right where we stand

Phaeax Forgive me, sir, that's not correct
  He wasn't pulled from the thigh here
  He was sewn into it.
  / Zeus gestated the foetal god –

Theseus Dionysus comes from Thebes
  That's what I'm saying

Phaeax Yes sir

Theseus Have they got plumbing here?

Talthybia We've been installing it. No hot water but

Theseus I like my water cold.
  So this is Thebes
  You can almost smell the history

Eurydice is dressing. Ismene attends her.

Eurydice First, I will express my disbelief

Ismene In what?

Eurydice Disbelief they voted for us
  I can't believe it

Ismene Well, they did

Eurydice I only fought because there had to be an
opposition
  We could not let the violence go on
  Could not have another Polynices
  So I found myself –
  It's literally like that
  Found myself with others
  Acting to oppose
  Speaking
  Words issuing from out my mouth
  In torrents
  A solace from the pain
  I never dreamt that politics would be my path
  I've always hated them
  Hated standing there at Creon's side
  Watching the ebb and flow of power from man to man
  The little games of consequence
  Experiments with human lives.
  Politics is what I've always fought against.
  But now I've won
  I'm feeling sick
  I've promised them pipe dreams, Ismene

Ismene You've promised peace

Eurydice I'm feeling I might actually throw up

Ismene Well, if you do, please miss the outfit

Eurydice Creon had principles until he was in power.
I saw what power did to him.
I watched the man diminish as it took its hold.
I watched his hopes and values all corrode

Ismene The people know you're different

Eurydice Am I, though?
Am I?
What will it do to me?
Ismene

Ismene Yes

Eurydice I'm meeting Theseus

Ismene I know; it's so exciting

Eurydice I look awful in this dress

Ismene I haven't finished yet
You need accessories
A scarf, you see?
Connotations of humility
But powerful mystique.
It softens all your lines
And then the architecture works

Eurydice Oh yes

Ismene You need an elegant but manly watch
To show that Time is your new god

Eurydice I love you

Ismene What about a bag?

Eurydice No bag

Ismene Athenians all have them
This one is designer

Eurydice I'm walking out into a world of men
    Unadorned and empty-handed

Ismene holds her.

Ismene Bring us justice

Aglaea enters.

Aglaea He is here

Eurydice I'm ready

Aglaea You have made a terrible mistake

Eurydice Don't you like it?

Aglaea You have not invited Sparta

Eurydice Oh

Aglaea I assumed you'd have the sense to see they must
be here

Eurydice If I invite the Spartans, Theseus might leave. I'll
not antagonise him

Aglaea We need Sparta or he'll walk all over you. We
need a bidding war with Thebes as prize –

Eurydice Athens stands for everything we've fought for:
freedom and democracy –

Aglaea For their own citizens

Eurydice Sparta is secretive, oppressive and aggressive
    They want an empire here by stealth –

Aglaea So does Theseus
    We are staring at the Titans
    Monsters both –
    Both poised to scavenge us.
    Be practical
    We have to play them
    One against the other

Eurydice That's a dangerous game for novices

Aglaea It's the only way we stand to win.
   We need money, not ideals
   Stability will only come with economic growth

Eurydice I will not get into bed with a regime
   That uses fear and violence to control.
   In Athens human rights are shrined in law

Aglaea They are a luxury
   When we have food enough / and sanitation

Eurydice Our principles won us this election
   And in the ruins of this bleeding state
   They are the only shreds of dignity we have.
   I put my trust in Theseus – on principle

Aglaea Then go and kiss his hairy hand

Eurydice I'm sorry that we disagree

Aglaea Nice dress

   She starts to go.

Be careful please
   I know he wears a splendid suit
   Sewn with a democratic thread;
   He's still a warlord with a warlord's heart

Eurydice All men are not so

Aglaea He fights his wars behind a desk
   But don't imagine that the beast is tame

Euphrosyne Eurydice, they've found a body by the walls.
It is the corpse of Polynices

   Eurydice and Ismene are profoundly affected.

Eurydice How do you know?

Euphrosyne His necklace

Eurydice I must see him

Euphrosyne Come, child

Aglaea Don't keep Theseus waiting

Eurydice (*going*) Nothing takes precedence

Eurydice and Euphrosyne exit.

Aglaea Is this the way it goes?
  Already she has put her own needs first

Ismene Polynices killed her son

Aglaea I know

Ismene My cousin Menoceus. He was only just thirteen

Aglaea I know

Ismene Polynices pulled the brains from out his skull
while still he lived –

Aglaea Yes, Ismene, yes
  But it is past.
  Her job is to secure our future

Ismene Why don't you go and meet him?

Aglaea Because I am incapable of hiding what I think
  And I think Theseus a bag of wind

SCENE THREE

Theseus enters with Talthybia and Phaeax.

Theseus So on a scale of one to ten, exactly how fucked
is this place?

Talthybia I'd say it's been up to eleven.
  Thebes is conflict-devastated

Theseus Currently around?

Talthybia Eight or nine
  Still very volatile

Theseus OK

Talthybia The election has improved things but there is
no infrastructure whatsoever; thousands of displaced,
traumatised people, destruction of homes, agriculture,
industry. The violence was bestial. There were seven
different armed militias all advancing on the city

Theseus I heard they ate each other

Talthybia Yes, combatants used to eat the brains of those
they killed in order to inherit strength and skill. Apparently
a custom from pre-Cadmus times. There has been
indescribable brutality. I put accounts into my briefing,
sir. Polynices said the violence would reshape the human
soul

Theseus You wrote that briefing?

Talthybia Yes sir

Theseus What's your name again?

Talthybia Talthybia

Theseus That's right; nice piece of work, Talthybia

Talthybia Thank you

Theseus It almost put me off my in-flight meal

Talthybia May I say, on behalf of everybody working on
the ground, how very glad we are to see you. Your visit's
a terrific boost to our morale

Theseus They have democracy and now they can rise out
of this disgusting quagmire

Talthybia That is our hope

Theseus So when do we begin to pull our peacekeepers out?

Phaeax In ten days' time

Talthybia But sir –

Phaeax Where is the president elect? She should be here by now.

> ELSEWHERE: *Eurydice is staring at Polynices' corpse. Euphrosyne and the soldiers accompany. She cannot tear her eyes away.*

Talthybia It's probably some urgent matter

Phaeax She can have no conception of your status, sir

Euphrosyne What shall we do with him?

Talthybia It's my belief that Thebes will need our presence here long term. There's a tremendous will for change but it won't happen overnight. In Eurydice, the people have chosen a leader / who –

Theseus Who is not here

Eurydice Do nothing
Let me think

Phaeax This is clearly someone, sir, with no experience

Talthybia She has experienced a decade of extreme and bloody war. When Creon died, the generals put her under house arrest. And even from her prison here she fought. She gave her strength to this amazing movement of women all risking their lives for peace

Theseus The women, right

Talthybia They would congregate in numbers and place themselves in the line of fire. During the peace talks they barricaded all the men inside the building, shamed them into peace. I find it deeply moving, inspirational

Theseus Yes, quite so

Talthybia She's given people hope.

Eurydice Polynices

Talthybia The leaders of this grass-roots movement; they are now the government

ELSEWHERE: *Eurydice and Euphrosyne exit.*

Phaeax The Minister of Finance was a teacher in a rural school

Talthybia Yes; she's incorruptible
She's sweeping out the toads, the ghosts, the layabouts
She'll spend our money on the people not on palaces and cars

Theseus There's no such thing as incorruptible

Talthybia Eurydice has said that everything must change.
The men have shown what they can do for Thebes
And now the women will

Phaeax Whoa

Theseus But what do we think; do we trust her?

Talthybia Yes I think / she's –

Theseus Do we like her?

Talthybia – very good news

Theseus Because she isn't here. Why is that?

Tiresias Welcome, blind traveller

Theseus I'm sorry?

Tiresias is with Harmonia. She holds out a hand for money.

Phaeax What's this person doing here?

Tiresias Welcome to the country of the blind

Phaeax I thought we had secured this area

Talthybia He's a beggar. That's his place. We've checked
him and he's not a threat. Don't look so scared; you don't
have to give him anything

Theseus I don't have any Theban currency

Talthybia The begging's kind of overwhelming – so I've
developed strategies. I only give to grandmothers; they're
the poorest and most selfless. Sometimes I give to
exceptionally hideous amputees but –

Theseus That is a grandmother

Talthybia No sir, excuse me; that's a man

Theseus It's a woman

Tiresias Give me your hand, King Theseus

Theseus Actually my title is First Citizen. We don't have
kings in Athens; we're a democratic state

Tiresias The future holds my clear unblinking gaze
　　It's only in the present that I'm blind.
　　Why don't you let me tell you what I see?

Theseus Female, unquestionably

Talthybia Male

Tiresias I'm both.
　　I saw two serpents mating on a path

Talthybia We have no interest, sorry

Tiresias (*taking Theseus' hand*) Intertwined
　　Encoiled, jaws wrapped round each other
　　Poison dripping in mistrust even as
　　They slithered propagation

Theseus Oh, OK

Tiresias The sight disgusted me. It seemed too human.
  I tore the slippery beasts apart
  And crushed one with my heel. It was the she.
  As punishment the snakes made me a woman

Theseus The snakes changed you into a woman?

Tiresias No punishment, say I, to be a female.
  Lying back, my legs spread wide, I know
  Ten times the bliss I suffered as a man.
  We suffer pleasure as we suffer pain
  You know this to be true. So does your wife

Theseus My wife?

Tiresias She's young; you married her last year

Theseus Good guess

Tiresias She harbours love for someone else.
  She doesn't want to but it's there, a love.
  It grows in her like cancer day by day.
  It will consume her

  Theseus pulls back his hand, deeply affected.

Theseus What the fuck?

Talthybia He's just a bullshit beggar, sir

  Harmonia holds out her hand for money.

Move along now please. You get him out of here

  Eurydice enters with Euphrosyne.

Theseus I want internet, hot water. I don't care if you
drag the generator up the hill yourself. I want a private
line, Phaedra on the end of it. And where's the fucking
president elect? I've flown all the way from Athens to
witness her inauguration and she doesn't have the
decency to meet me

Eurydice Theseus
Hello

Eurydice takes his hand.

Welcome to Thebes

Theseus Eurydice

Eurydice We're thrilled to see you
Thank you so much for coming.
It means a great deal to Thebes and to me

Theseus Congratulations on your victory

Eurydice Thank you. My late husband Creon was a great
admirer of all things Athenian. So am I, especially
democracy

Theseus That's good to hear
You look smaller than your photograph

Eurydice So do you
Let me walk you round our gardens. Miraculously they
survived the war – and they're so cool at this time of the
day. Do you have humming birds in Athens?

They exit, followed by the aides, bodyguards.
Talthybia gives Harmonia some money.

Talthybia (*to Tiresias*) So what about me? Will you tell
me my life?

Tiresias I cannot see you

Talthybia I'm here. What's my destiny, old man?

Tiresias You are a faceless nameless minion. You don't
have one

SCENE FOUR

Haemon, Eunomia and Senator Thalia enter. Haemon's eyes have suffered serious injury. They approach Polykleitos, a mechanic.

Thalia My name is Thalia, I'm a senator of your new government. We're here collecting testimony

Polykleitos So I've heard

Thalia Would you like to contribute?
  It's so important that we speak
  That we are heard

Polykleitos You are evangelists, I think

Haemon Evangelists for truth and reconciliation

Thalia These are my trainees

Polykleitos What happened to your eyes?

Haemon Nothing
  They met some flying masonry
  At high velocity
  I was a student doctor
  Now I'm this
  Haemon

Polykleitos Polykleitos
  Forgive me if I ask what good will speaking do?

Eunomia Thalia's been taking testimony since the massacre

Thalia Before the war I was a social worker

Eunomia Now she's been elected Minister of Justice

Thalia I care about that word. I want to see it done

Polykleitos Forgive me if I say I've heard it all before

Haemon If this country is to heal, we have to start a dialogue between the victims of the violence and its perpetrators

Thalia We hear you've suffered loss

Polykleitos Truth and reconciliation: pretty words

Thalia We have to give them meaning, make them actions

Polykleitos I've been working for the Athenians
As mechanic
Dismantling these weapons
It feels good.
Turn on your machine

Haemon starts recording.

Before the war I had a garage
My son and me were hiding in the store.
In other countries, children are a precious thing.
In Thebes they have no value.
I can't vomit up the words

Thalia Each child's death should bring this city to a halt
I lost my daughter in this war

Polykleitos I spent my life in service to the gods
Not in service no, in contemplation of the mystery
I thought there was an order to the universe
When I looked up at the sky at night
I'd see a pattern mathematical in its complexity
Now I see random dots
There's nothing
But
An image like a bloodstain
Of the soldiers
Roaring through our streets.
A man broke down our door

Haemon Do you remember when, which faction, which attack on Thebes?

Polykleitos I know exactly who he was
   That's why I'm speaking here.
   He took my son and –

ELSEWHERE: *Prince Tydeus enters.*

Tydeus OK that's enough, don't look at them; you look at me. I'm more enlightening than anything that's going on there. That is sad old shit. Truth and reconciliation? That is sell-your-neighbour by a different name. That is make up lies about the people you don't like and get them tried for war crimes. I bet I'm being blamed for every murder here in Thebes and none of it is true, no, none of it. I am Prince Tydeus. Not a royal one; my mother brought me up to run her pig farm, actually; it's just that Prince is quite a common name in Thebes – a lot of mothers like to have a little Prince. But I was never going to spend my life with swine. The gods had better plans for me. Now here are three true facts. One: I am a first-class athlete. I have wiped the floor with all the best of Athens and with Sparta. I have won first prize at the Nemean Games. You can see my winning javelin throw on my own website – one of the first in Thebes – designed by the woman I adore, who understands domains

   Senator Pargeia enters.

Kids have posters of me on their walls draped in the flag of Thebes – Prince Tydeus: gold. Two: I have had communication with the gods

Pargeia That's true
   The Prince first saw Dionysus when he was just a little boy

Tydeus I didn't see
   It's more like I became

Pargeia You hear that?
  He becomes
  Like in that movie where the man puts on the mask

Tydeus Not quite like that
  I felt him in me when I won that gold;
  Felt him moving in me
  When I led my men through Thebes.
  I feel his light within my heart, my brain
  I hear his holy laugh come out my mouth
  I'll tell you this
  Dionysus is a very complex god.
  He doesn't choose just anyone.
  Three: I fought for justice and for peace

Pargeia That's right. He fought for Polynices

Tydeus He was rightful heir in Thebes and he should be
running it right now. Polynices taught me everything
I know. He was more like a brother than a friend. This is
his wife, Pargeia

Pargeia Hi

Tydeus I was just telling them about your skill with
websites and domains

Pargeia That's nice

Tydeus This woman is a true-life heroine. Not only is she
beautiful –

Pargeia Now now

Tydeus – but she is clever and she's full of heart

Pargeia During the war years, while I worked as loan
advisor at the Bank of Thebes, I used my post to raise
funds for the orphans

Tydeus Any other information you might hear about her
finances is quite unfuckingtrue

Pargeia My husband, Polynices, should be ruling Thebes.
But he –
  I'm sorry –

Tydeus He's among the disappeared

Pargeia No he is not 'among'. He is unique. He has
uniquely gone. He led his men into the whirlwind of the
fight and then –
  Forgive me –

Tydeus He has not been seen

Pargeia Tydeus is my best support
  My truest Prince
  He has sat with me through my hours of grief
  The torment of not knowing –

Tydeus Rumour is that Polynices is residing in the forest,
biding time

Pargeia Zeus transported him to safety

Tydeus We like to think his jeep was swallowed by the
gods of death and now he is beneath the earth

Pargeia Gathering unworldly power

Tydeus Ready to be spewed back up into the face of
Thebes and take, by force, what's his

Pargeia We stood for him in this election
  Prince Tydeus

Tydeus The man with god inside

Pargeia Our policies were strong
  Firm leadership
  Security for all those on our side

Tydeus But then we lost
  It's inconfuckingceivable
  We're merely senators

Pargeia Which only goes to show how pointless an election is

Thalia approaches.

Thalia Senator Tydeus

Tydeus That is Prince to you

She hands him a document.

Thalia The Truth and Reconciliation Commission of Thebes requests you to appear before it to address yourself to allegations of war crimes and gross human rights violations during the course of the Theban civil war. Failure to attend will result in compulsory subpoena and criminal prosecution. (*To Pargeia.*) Good morning to you, Senator Pargeia. I hear they are investigating loan frauds at the Bank of Thebes. Have a lovely day

She exits.

Pargeia Hold back
  Resist the rage

Tydeus Oh fuck democracy. I hate the whole idea of it
  We've got enough arms left to take the compound
  And the palace –

Pargeia Do I need to say it twice? Hold back
  Sweet Prince
  Sometimes you are an innocent.
  There are much better ways to fuck those bitches up
  One: we need the people on our side
  Two: we need the influence of Theseus

Tydeus When I look at you
  It's like I feel the god
  Rising up in me

He tries to kiss her. Antigone enters.

Pargeia No. Not while my husband Polynices lives
I want to
But I can't

She sees Antigone, who is looking at her strangely.

Pargeia What is it, sister?

Antigone Nothing

Pargeia I don't like the way you look at me
Like I'm not good enough
To be your brother's wife
And I have proved my worth
On my feet and on my back
Please tell me what your problem is

Antigone The dead see everything we do

Pargeia exits.

Tydeus Oedipus' daughters
There are two
The mad one and the cute one.
This one's mad.

He exits

Act Two

SCENE ONE

Antigone remains. Ismene enters.

Ismene What are you doing? What's the matter?

Antigone They found Polynices. Dead

Ismene I know
Antigone

Antigone I went to look at him.
His eyes were no longer eyes
Open right into the deep

Ismene He's dead and gone
It's over

*As they speak, the stage is being prepared for the
inauguration.*

Antigone I'm going to anoint the corpse with oil
Come with me

Ismene But it's Eurydice's inauguration

Antigone Why should I care for that?

Ismene She wants us with her, by her side

The company are entering and taking up position.

Antigone But he's our brother

Ismene You never lived with him. I did
You were on the road with Oedipus for all those years
And you were spared

Antigone Spared? Out there in the war zone with our
dying father?

31

Ismene Polynices was a cunning, red-eyed despot
And this palace was a prison under him.
He used to pick up women from the town
And bring them here to play with and to rape.
You ask Eurydice. She hated him –

Antigone I don't care what he did

Ismene He let his generals
High on heroin and gunpowder
He let dogs like Prince Tydeus –

Antigone I've heard the stories same as you

Ismene Stories?

Antigone I've heard about his necklace made of fingers

Ismene I hated him

Antigone He is our blood

Ismene I won't go back
The war is over

Antigone Not until we've buried all the dead.
I've noticed in these days of peace how soon you have
concerned yourself with what to wear, with grooming,
painting of your toes –

Ismene We have survived
Survived our lives so far.
Why not start living them?

Antigone cracks into tears.

Antigone We have to bury him
He frightens me

Ismene embraces her.
The company enters, Tydeus and Pargeia making a flamboyant show.

Tydeus Senators, good morning

Eris What are you doing here?

Pargeia We are elected representatives of Thebes

Tydeus We're here to offer hospitality to Theseus

Helia There's something here that you don't understand

Euphrosyne Called politics

Thalia We won the votes
We are the government
You lost
You are the opposition

Pargeia So?

Eunomia You're not invited

Aglaea Senators, your place is over there

Pargeia and Tydeus retreat to their positions. A rousing national anthem. The Athenians join in, unsure of tune or words. Eurydice and Theseus enter.

Anthem
In the towns and our plain lands
In the heart of our Thebes
The road to peace and freedom
Is a path for us all
For we will build a new world
Our nation will be reborn
And feel the pride of our plain lands
In the heart of our Thebes

Eurydice stands at a podium, Theseus at her side.
Antigone tries to leave. Ismene holds her back. At last Antigone acquiesces.
The anthem ends. Antigone, an oddity among the dignitaries, keeps her head bowed.

Eurydice Thebans, war is over. We are free
How happy it makes me to say that.
Let me say it again loud and clear:
People of Thebes, we are free.
This is truly a wonderful day.
I stand before you, leader of our new democracy.
My first task is to thank you
Thank you for believing Thebes can rise again
And thank you for believing in
This Theban woman. She believes in you.
I want to talk to the women here
The women in this city turned the tide for peace,
Women put themselves in danger
Walked wearing white in front of guns,
Nagged and pleaded, begged and laboured
Advocated tirelessly, withheld sexual favours
And never gave up. Women gave us peace.
This new administration will reflect their courage.
Women will be given prominence at every level.
Euphrosyne, Minister of Finance
Thalia, Minister of Justice
Aglaea, Foreign Secretary
Bia, Trade and Industry
Helia, Agriculture
Eris, Chief of Police
And men, we love you too:
Xenophanes, Education
We have senators reflecting all opinions here
Some radically different from my own.
We'll learn to listen, compromise and bend
We'll learn the skills of peace
Here, to share our celebration
Theseus, First Citizen of Athens

Theseus There is excitement in the air.
I can hear it, Thebans, feel it.
Like the rhythm of your famous music,

I find it irresistible. As I look down
Upon your city streets and out across
Your towns and fertile plains
I see you all rebuilding homes
Mending roads, reconstructing life.
I'm honoured to be witness at the birth of this
democracy. When I return next time, I hope to see an
open governmental infrastructure, functioning without
corruption. I hope to see the rule of law. I hope to see a
land where business thrives, endeavour is rewarded, and
stability achieved. If peace is maintained, Athens and her
partners could do business here. Imagine this: a vast
economic development zone, bringing investment and
employment; industry that would transform your land.
The quality is there, the opportunity, the will. Your war is
over. Now improve yourselves. Thank you

Eurydice In our hope for the peace, let us not forget the
war.
Thebes has been witness to atrocities
That I can hardly heave into my mouth
We have seen butchery and slaughter
Our girls raped, boys brutalised with guns.
What meaning can we find in that?
The only meaning is to make a lasting peace.
We have lost children, parents, brothers, sisters
I lost my husband Creon, Menoceus my youngest son,
My eldest, Haemon, blinded here

Haemon Not blind

Eurydice I fought with grief through the long night
And in your faces I can see its shadow.
I want to remember those we have lost.
Please join me in two minutes' silence

Tiresias marks the beginning of the silence.
All bow their heads. For the first time, Antigone

raises hers. About thirty seconds pass. Tydeus falls to his knees. He speaks in a high voice.

Tydeus People – for you I died
  A long time I lay in darkness
  Then the plates of my skull came apart

Pargeia The dead speak

Tydeus My spirit breathed
  Began to rise
  It ploughed the night sky
  Searching for the hidden side
  That keeps Elysium from human eyes
  But far below where lies the plain of Thebes
  There came a roar of souls
  Thebes
  We mourn for you
  The dead are grieving
  You have been robbed of strength
  Your power is lost in woman's hands
  Look to the P—
  To the P—

Pargeia Look to the P—

Tydeus feigns collapse.

Tiresias The dead are all around
  You make a mockery of them
  You deafen them

Tiresias marks the end of the silence.

Thalia You have insulted the dead

Euphrosyne You shameless fake

Eurydice I know that violent men still lurk
  Trying to spin their dark ideas aflame.
  But while we breathe we will resist them
  / And we will not let you down

Pargeia Our ancestors are grieving
  Thebes, her promises are hollow
  / Eurydice can't keep control

Eurydice I will not let you oppress and silence me

Pargeia / Polynices is true leader
  You are standing in our place

Eurydice Your president, people of Thebes
  Will not be bullied or harassed

Theseus Listen now
  This is a democracy
  And everybody gets a chance to speak.
  That is what you have a senate for

Pargeia Beloved Theseus, the dead have spoken here

Tydeus Who did they die for?
  Not Eurydice, not this

Pargeia They died for Polynices

Tydeus / Don't betray the Theban dead
  Revolt against this government of women

Eurydice I did not march into the guns of violent men
  To then be cowed by them.
  I will speak. I will speak. I will speak.
  To reconcile does not mean to forget.
  We must never forget,
  Lest we make the same mistakes again.
  Polynices' body has been found.
  It will not be given burial

  Antigone steps forward. Pargeia almost collapses.

Eurydice This warlord's corpse shall be our monument
  To all the horrors we have witnessed / and survived

Pargeia If you don't bury him his soul will walk / the
earth

Eurydice His violent ideology will decompose –
  As peace grows up and / overwhelms it

Pargeia (*to Tydeus*) The voice that spoke through / you –

Eurydice The ground where he / lies

Pargeia He used you as his / vessel

Eurydice It will be a garden of / reflection
  Where we can meditate upon the cost of war

Tydeus People, to the square, come now
  Come in your multitudes
  If you have human feeling then oppose this wrong

Pargeia Polynices

  Pargeia's distress is epic. Tydeus escorts her out.

Eurydice I love Thebes
  I see light. I see water
  I see the terror melting like ice
  Let us turn away from shadows.
  If you oppose me, tell me democratically.
  Work hard for peace
  Be part of this great effort
  Join hands, be free

Theseus May I?

Eurydice Thank you.

  Theseus leads Eurydice down from the podium.

Antigone Her first act
  As lord, as queen

Ismene As democratically / elected –

Antigone As all-powerful ruler is to let our brother rot

Ismene Antigone

Theseus An interesting speech, ma'am

Ismene She is not the monster

Eurydice Thank you

Ismene Don't go

Theseus I should offer you the service of my writing team. They're very good at rousing with the facts

Eurydice That's very kind

Theseus You know, an expert on language and the human brain said that women find rhetoric more difficult

Eurydice Thank you very much for telling me

Theseus I mean, next time, before you go up there, you could run your stuff by my professionals to see if there's improvements to be made / because

Eurydice I write my own words, thank you. My late husband Creon said it was statesmanship

Theseus Statesmanship, that's nice. That decomposing corpse

Eurydice Polynices

Theseus You should have run that by me

Eurydice I didn't know the dead were an Athenian concern. Forgive my inexperience

Theseus (*to Phaeax*) The possessed guy

Phaeax That was Prince Tydeus: electoral opponent

Theseus And she?

Phaeax Senator Pargeia. She's the corpse's wife

Talthybia You'll find detailed profiles of them in my briefing, sir

Phaeax She used to be a dancer

Theseus Fascinating

Phaeax He's the guy who won at the Nemean Games

Theseus Impassioned, isn't he?

Phaeax His record for the javelin still stands

Theseus OK. His name again?

Phaeax Tydeus

Theseus The Prince. (*To Eurydice.*) He is a tough adversary

Eurydice Yes, and so am I.
  This is my son, Haemon

Theseus How do you do?

Haemon I started my medical training in Athens;
beautiful city

Theseus Certainly is

Haemon I mean what are your plans?
  Sorry to jump on you like this but
  Healthcare provision
  We need drugs, buildings, trained staff
  / It's critical that –

Phaeax The provision of medical aid is a topic for
discussion at conference. It will receive our full attention
then

Theseus What happened to your eyes?

Haemon Nothing

Eurydice He was / injured

Haemon I've suffered certain functional changes but –

Eurydice He's blind

Haemon Why do you keep –
    I'm not blind.
    I can see your dress
    That thing you're wearing on your head
    I can see Antigone

He is pointing at Ismene.

My sight is just impaired

Theseus That happen in the war?

Haemon In the peace
    Clearing rubble from our disused university
    One of the factions had it booby-trapped with mines

Theseus I'm very sorry

Haemon Yes. They were Athenian made

Eurydice Haemon

Haemon That's the irony, you see. Thebes is not a
weapons-manufacturing state. Most of the arms in our
conflict were / Athenian

Eurydice My nieces: Ismene, Antigone

Theseus Your father was Oedipus, right?

Ismene That's right

Antigone Our father and our brother

He shakes Ismene's hand.

Theseus Yes. I feel I'm shaking hands with someone
destiny has touched. You're Antigone?

Ismene Ismene

Theseus There are some families like that
    Families who get touched by destiny
    Chosen in some way –
    Don't you think so?

Antigone / Yes

Ismene No, I don't

Eurydice My cabinet in waiting; Euphrosyne, Minister of Finance

Phaeax The teacher

Euphrosyne How do you do?

Theseus My pleasure

Euphrosyne I have the honour of holding the purse strings of a bankrupt state. I've explored the lining of this purse in case a coin or two is hiding there but all I've found is fluff and old receipts

Theseus That's too bad

Euphrosyne I also have a cheque for you: the latest instalment of interest on the overwhelming debts we have inherited. Would you like it?

Phaeax Debt relief is down on the agenda but there are various criteria you must fulfil and now is not the time to list them

Phaeax doesn't take the cheque.

Eurydice Eris, Chief of Police

Theseus How do you –

Eris We're going to have the rule of law here
But we need to retrain, reorganise
We can make Thebes safe
But we need your cash

Eurydice Xenophanes, Education

Theseus Very nice to –

Xenophanes We have to re-educate our men
A generation now thinks rape and looting is their right.

Education is the road to change
But it's expensive –

Eurydice Thalia, Minister of Justice

Thalia We have so much to talk about. A just society –
how is that achievable?

Theseus Well –

Thalia I hope that Thebes can learn from your mistakes

Euphrosyne He looks like a movie star, doesn't he?

Thalia You have the figure and the bearing of a very
gifted actor

Eurydice Aglaea, Foreign Minister

Theseus How do you do?

Aglaea We met before. I came to Athens just before the
massacre to plead for intervention

Theseus That's right

Aglaea Sadly it was not forthcoming

Eurydice We've arranged a Theban feast. We hope you'll
join us

Phaeax Sir, our caterers have worked alongside theirs to
ensure health and hygiene

Theseus Thank you, Madam President

*Eurydice and Theseus exit with Phaeax and the
senators.*

Talthybia (*to Aglaea*) I have to say it isn't wise. Please
tell your people. Don't make Theseus feel that he's at
fault. He didn't make this war

They exit. Ismene and Antigone alone.

Antigone I'm going to bury him, Ismene

Ismene Can't you see there's something more important going on?

Antigone His soul can't rest

Ismene If you bury him now you'll be siding with Tydeus and the widow

Antigone / No I won't

Ismene They'll leap on you like a trophy. / They'll use you, Antigone

Antigone This has got nothing to do with Prince Tydeus or anyone else

Ismene It has to do with all of Thebes. We have to be so careful

Antigone Why?

Ismene Because of who we are

Antigone Last remnants of a cursed house

Ismene I want to represent the future, not the past. We must embrace this peace

Antigone Eurydice isn't peace
       She's power
       Power is never peace
       It is barbarity.
       Come with me

Ismene Why don't we talk to her?
       She's not / unreasonable

Antigone What good did talking ever do?
       The only thing to do is act – and you
       Have never done
       Anything

*Haemon enters. They both look at him; Ismene with
a certain amount of hope.*

Haemon Antigone?

Ismene immediately leaves.

Where are you going? Don't go

Antigone I'm here

Haemon My mother asks if you'll come in and join the
feast

Antigone I'm not hungry

Haemon Antigone

Antigone Don't come too near

Haemon Why not?

Antigone I'm ill

Haemon What with?

Antigone Don't know

Haemon I know what I must seem; how especially
Disgusting my fading sight must seem

Antigone To me?

Haemon I wish it was an arm or leg
But it's my eyes. My images of you
Are stuck now in the past. I doubt I'll see
Your face again, though I imagine it.
Are you still there?

Antigone Yes

Haemon It's common to feel
Paranoid like that, they say.
I think that I see people creep away.
They've warned me of hallucinations too.

I might see any nonsense, any lie
And take it for what's real. Don't go

Antigone I'm not

Haemon This is a minor injury in Theban terms –

Antigone You're not especially disgusting
Why did you say that?

Haemon Before I went to Athens I remember you
Leading your blind father
Seeing for him, so small
You were like a bird
Taking him where you found interest
Even if he didn't want to go.
I loved to watch.
You were a proper child
You had a playful spirit
Your smile could penetrate his blindness
Wrap itself around his grief
You were his light, Antigone.
I've always felt it when I looked at you
Some kind of light
Don't know why
You're scrawny, awkward
Not like Ismene, she is radiant I'd say, but you
You're like a flare burning through the night.
Since I've been like this it's you I've seen
Your face, your eyes, those eyes

He reaches out for her.

Are you still here?

Antigone I thought it was Ismene that you loved

Haemon It's you

They touch.

Antigone I'm dangerous to touch

Haemon Like fire

Antigone I'm ill

Haemon What with?

Antigone Don't know

Haemon Do you feel anything for me?

Antigone No

Suddenly she is in his arms.

Haemon I knew
 I knew you did

Antigone Help me

Haemon Antigone

SCENE TWO

Late at night. Miletus, Scud and Megaera are guarding the body of Polynices. Harmonia is quietly singing.

Megaera More dishonest work for warriors to do

Miletus If we're told to sit here with a stiff, we sit with it. That way we get fed

Scud This kid that I was with
 Don't know his name but he was small
 A green militia came with faces painted white
 We found him lying there
 After the bullets and the fight
 His life had gone – but there was not a scratch on him

Megaera Another dead-kid story from the Junior Lieutenant

Scud He died of fear the big men said
    And they pissed on him.
    I didn't know that it was possible
    To die from fear
    He followed us for some time after that
    And he was grey.
    Once he touched me on the back

Megaera That's nice of him. That's friendly, isn't it? Shut up

Eurydice and Theseus lead the company out from dinner.

Eurydice When Cadmus founded Thebes
    He laid Harmonia, his beloved, in their bed
    And drew the seven gates around her
    Taking his inspiration from the seven heavens.
    Thebes is laid out like a celestial map

Theseus That's poetic. Athens is a grid

Eurydice Our districts have the names of constellations
    That's Lyra Town down there
    And over here on the hill is the spring where Cadmus killed the giant serpent

Theseus Wow

Eurydice He threw its teeth on the ground and warriors sprang up
    They helped him build the city

Eurydice and Theseus move away, followed by Phaeax, aides, bodyguards and senators. Thalia, Euphrosyne and Bia remain.

Thalia She's doing very well

Bia That charm of hers. She makes it look so easy

Thalia Perhaps it is to her

Euphrosyne These Athenians. We speak the same language, we have the same gods, but they're so hard to talk to. I felt like an anthropologist in there.

Helia They've got no sense of humour

Euphrosyne I was with that aide

Helia Oh, he's a nightmare

Euphrosyne I couldn't think of anything to say
I started talking about grandchildren
His eyes glazed over straight away
I found myself describing the destruction of my village
The food stayed on his plate
Then I remembered sport –
Thank the gods, he talked for half an hour

Thalia That girl with the stiff hair –

Bia Talthybia

Helia She knocked her drink into her lap

Thalia Poor thing
She asked so many questions
I was actually impressed
I think she's a bit in love with Theseus

Bia So am I

Euphrosyne Well, I'm sorry to inform you that he has a wife

Bia No match for me

Aglaea enters.

Euphrosyne A beautiful young wife: Phaedra. Their wedding was all over the celebrity sites on the internet. Of course I never look at them. But her dress: so many little precious stones sewn into the organza. You could open several schools for what it cost

49

Aglaea Can't we rise above the gossip?

Euphrosyne This isn't gossip, this is economics

Aglaea Listen
That's Pargeia and the Prince down in the square
I've told Eris to stand by with her police
What if there's trouble and they can't contain it?

Thalia We have the peacekeepers
It's what they're here for

Bia We'll go and talk to their security

Bia and Helia exit.

Euphrosyne I don't think Tydeus will attempt a coup
while Theseus is here

Aglaea Tydeus wants to show him we're unstable and
incapable
He wants to show we're overwhelmed / by the task

Euphrosyne Overwhelmed but undaunted. We're
planting seeds, her ladies – tiny seeds that will grow and
change the land.

Thalia The Athenians are pulling out in ten days' time.
We have to have assurances of aid and debt relief.
Eurydice has got to sell us hard

Aglaea How I hate the fact that we need Theseus.
That speech of his
It made me livid
Telling us we could improve ourselves
As if we're children learning how to spell
And offering the carrot of his economic zone

Euphrosyne He's got to feed the great Athenian god: the
god of profit

Aglaea And Eurydice – I'm sorry but I'm furious.

What was she thinking of – to leave that corpse exposed
without discussion and without advice?

Euphrosyne Your voice is very loud

Aglaea That rabble in the square; she's given them the
gift of self-righteous indignation. What an error – and she
made it like an autocrat

Thalia You see the thing is, I appreciate her gesture.
There is poetry in it. I lost my daughter in this war

Aglaea I know, I know –

Thalia And that unburied monster –
 I know it wasn't him that raped and killed her
 But the fact that there's just one –
 Just one of those ferocious men
 Whose soul will never rest

Aglaea You're Minister of Justice

Thalia Yes, I think that it is just.
 His corpse is made to pay
 The dead make reparation
 While the living start to heal

Euphrosyne We have to show her loyalty

Aglaea What of her loyalty to us?
 We senators must act as a control on her great power

Euphrosyne We need her to have power.
 What good is honest, competent committee
 In the face of Prince Tydeus?
 He genuinely thinks that he's a god.
 And he is charismatic, handsome, plausible
 Especially with that glossy thief upon his arm.
 We're dull, we're ageing, we wear comfy footwear
 None of us is sexy any more
 We don't throw parties, we like gardening

Aglaea Tydeus and Pargeia have the crowd
We have to hope that when the food and beer runs out
Their cult of character will sour

Thalia We must have Theseus

Euphrosyne And to get him we need her, Eurydice
Her confidence, her charm, her gravitas
Her sense of her own right –

Aglaea Her pride

Euphrosyne Your pride

Thalia I feel we're holding floodgates closed
Exhausted with the weight
We have to be united. Please stand firm
Or the approaching rush
Will overwhelm us all

Euphrosyne The greatest threat to Thebes
Is Thebes itself

Phaeax and Enyalius enter with the senators.

Phaeax Excuse me, what is going on down there? I have
concerns for Theseus

Aglaea Keep calm
We should stand by
But not provoke
That way this little fire will burn itself right out

Exit aides and senators.

ELSEWHERE: *the revellers enter, carrying Tydeus on
their shoulders. Polykleitos watches from the shadows.*

Tydeus Breathe frenzy

Pargeia Prince Tydeus

*A chant starts up: 'Breathe frenzy, Prince Tydeus.'
Polykleitos raises a gun, aims it at Tydeus.*

Pargeia Fill your stomach, feed your flesh, let your hair down, breathe frenzy, free your senses, cry joy and feel the god

Tydeus Breathe frenzy

Polykleitos cannot pull the trigger. He lowers the gun. The revellers exit.

ELSEWHERE: *Talthybia is with Ismene.*

Talthybia I've drunk too much

Ismene Me too

Talthybia What is that stuff, that wine?

Ismene Not really wine. It's made out of fermented bread

Talthybia Oh, fermented

Theseus enters. He is on his mobile phone.

Theseus Can you do something for me please?
Call in on your mother? Yes, I know she is;
I mean on Phaedra, she's your mother now

Talthybia Great sky

Ismene You have the same sky over Athens

Theseus I'm only asking you to see if she's OK
She hasn't been returning calls
I don't know what she's doing there

Talthybia Our sky's polluted with a smog of light.
We have an orange glow; couple of white dots
/ But that is just spectacular. That path

Theseus I'm worried that –
Just go
Find out why she's there. And privately –

Ismene Oh yes, the path of stars

Theseus You keep it in the family. Thanks

Talthybia At first I thought it was a kind of high cloud cover but this Theban guy I met who dismantles guns and weapons said it's actually –

Polykleitos (*elsewhere*) / The Milky Way

Talthybia – the Milky Way

Ismene That's right

Talthybia I didn't know. He said our star, the sun –

Polykleitos Is on an outer spur of a great spiral of the galaxy

Talthybia – and the Milky Way

Polykleitos Or silver river, is our view of the
    Galactic plane going right into the crux
    Full of dust from old, exploded stars
    And ionising new ones – countless
    Suns and moons and planets, and it turns
    Through space at an amazing speed, not just
    A moon around an earth or earth round sun
    But all of it; the galaxy spins round

Talthybia And this mechanic guy said it's just one –

Polykleitos Of billions like it in the universe

Talthybia And at the centre of it all, guess what
    He was looking for?

Ismene A super-massive black hole

Talthybia No, not that. He said he wanted Heaven

Ismene Very nice

Polykleitos / Elysium

Talthybia Elysium; that was the word he used.
    He searches for Elysium

Ismene The centre of the galaxy is actually dark matter

Talthybia Oh. OK

Ismene It's going to eat us up

Theseus She's right. One day you'd better hope
　　You're on a space ship out of here

He laughs. No one else finds it funny. Eurydice enters;
Aglaea and Eris are briefing her.

I used to do a lot of sailing;
　　Love the night sky
　　And I'm appreciating what you said about dark matter
　　I've read a lot about black holes and stuff, Antigone.
　　Dark matter means we've got to make the most of
what's around

Aglaea and Eris exit. Eurydice approaches.

Eurydice We've had a small disturbance in the central
square
　　It's calming down

Theseus Your opposition, right?

Eurydice Just drunken revellers
　　Celebrating our democracy

Theseus Making their feelings known about the dead guy

Eurydice That is their democratic right

Theseus (*to Talthybia*) Could we get some music here?
　　I hate an evening without music

Ismene In Thebes we always make our own

She exits, with Talthybia.

Eurydice You don't like silence, Theseus?

Theseus You don't like music?

Eurydice Did you make your call?

Theseus Yes, thank you. My wife has left our place in Athens and she's heading for the coast. Why would she do that?

Eurydice I don't know

Theseus Hippolytus my son is stationed there with his battalion. I've asked him to go out and check on her

Eurydice That's very good of him

Theseus He doesn't like her. Not one bit.
I'm not entirely sure that he likes me

Eurydice Families can be very difficult

Theseus You lost a son, is that right?

Eurydice He
Down by the walls
Menoceus, my youngest.
In an ambush
He was –

Pause.

Theseus How did you lose your husband?

Eurydice On his way to Delphi at one of our outlying villages, his convoy was stopped at a roadblock. It was made of human intestines

Theseus No way

Eurydice They were massacred

Theseus By this Polynices?

Eurydice By his men. I don't think they knew who Creon was. They were just massacring everyone that day. But when they realised who they'd killed they – let's say they made full use of his remains

Theseus What happens when a whole state
   When a place descends into – fuck
   It's like you bred some different kind of war out here

Eurydice All war is savage, Theseus, whether it's fought
close quarters with machetes or from afar with missiles
and computer-guided bombs. Are you more civilised
because you can't hear people scream?

Theseus Your war was bestial

Eurydice Our war was very human

Theseus Then I fear a new breed of mankind. Men with
no feeling, no idea of order or regard for any tie, men
whose only motivation is the basest lust for power

Eurydice That's new?

Theseus The path we've been on for the last millennium
or so, the glory of the city state, philosophy and science,
freedom, art, enlightenment: the things that Athens
stands for. I believe in them and I had thought our
progress irreversible. I thought we would continue to
evolve towards the gods

Eurydice We're not evolving backwards here

Theseus What happened? How did this exterminating
butchery take hold?

Eurydice It could happen anywhere

Theseus You cannot say that

Eurydice Does it frighten you?
   Do you think we brought it on ourselves?
   It could happen anywhere where there is tyranny.
   You should go out and talk to people, talk
   As I have done to those who have endured.
   I'd say they were the finest human beings you could
meet.

What's happened here is in the past.
Perhaps you are afraid of us
Because the chaos here, the great descent
Just might be in your future

Theseus What the hell makes you say that?

Eurydice An observation, merely

*Ismene and Talthybia enter with a clockwork radio.
Music.*

Talthybia Some music, sir

Eurydice Thank you, Talthybia. Good night

Talthybia and Ismene exit.

Theseus I've made an observation too. You have a way
with people that I envy; got them wrapped around your
finger

Eurydice Have I?

Theseus You appear strong

Eurydice I'm motivated by necessity

Theseus You appear humane, intelligent, compassionate
and wise. But I'm not sure if you are

Eurydice Thebes knows what I stand for and the people
trust me to bring change. It's what I must do – or die
trying

Theseus That's so Theban, bringing death into every
sentence

Eurydice Death is everywhere in Thebes

Theseus Like your address; way too dramatic. Some of
the things you said

Eurydice I said we must reconcile

Theseus No, you said light and water and men lurking in the dark spinning fire

Eurydice All the most important things were said

Theseus This dead boy that you refuse to bury –

Eurydice The warlord who murdered my son

Theseus Where does he fit in to your reconciliation?

Eurydice I explained that in my speech

Theseus His corpse will be a theme park?

Eurydice Don't misinterpret me. It's vital to the healing of our wounds that he makes reparation. I've no desire to clash with you

Theseus Quite right

Eurydice But this is Theban business. You've no right to interfere

Theseus May I just say how well you argue and defend yourself. For someone new to government, you're good

Eurydice Thank you

Theseus You're also beautiful

Eurydice I – what?

Theseus That is so unusual in politics
    Not coming on to you; just stating a bare fact.
    Beauty is a very powerful thing.
    My wife is beautiful
    Phaedra: gets mistaken for my daughter.
    Don't know why I'm saying this
    Relief perhaps
    Of being with a woman my own age
    A clever, charming, deeply foreign woman

    Pause.

Eurydice Thank you but we have no electricity
No schools, no medicine, no roads
No jobs, no drinking water
Children dying in their droves
Our life expectancy is thirty-eight.
I'm old beyond my years

Theseus You don't look old.
I envy you, you know
Envy the adventure, the extremity
Our lives in Athens seem mundane
We have no tragedy. And tragedy
Reminds us how to live

Eurydice I'm glad it serves some purpose

Theseus Eurydice. You'll learn how rare it is to meet an equal

Eurydice Theseus, my hands are tied with monstrous poverty.
For Thebes to thrive where chaos gaped and roared
You can perform that miracle –

Theseus You see this is what I'm saying: metaphors and monsters. Gaped and roared: that's just verbose. It's / not effective

Eurydice What I have said is very clear. We need a future. You can / help us

Theseus You've just been elected.
I can see you're very keen.
You are a natural and I'm most impressed.
But sometimes late at night
When everything official has been said
We leaders of the world like to
Take off the mask
We've done the altruism and diplomacy.
Now let's do something else

Eurydice What would amuse you, Theseus?

Theseus Like look up at the stars
 And see what destiny might hold

Eurydice It's worrying that you don't listen. Is it something that the male brain has inadequate equipment for?

Theseus I do listen and I think you're so naive. There is a lot that I could do for Thebes

Eurydice Naive?

Theseus But let's remember that essentially you're begging here, you're on your knees

Eurydice That's what I've said. Thebes is / imprisoned by

Theseus Not Thebes; you. Every thousand that I pledge keeps you in power. I just offered you equality

Eurydice Did you?

Theseus I had a glimpse of something just back then
 Some sort of –
 Obviously not destiny, but say
 A door swinging open unexpectedly.
 This relationship with Thebes
 Could be a pleasure, not a chore

Eurydice Are you
 Are you suggesting
 That we presidents –

Theseus I'm not a president. I'm just First Citizen

Eurydice That's right, the common man

Theseus Dionysus – he was born here, wasn't he, the god of wine? Don't you women have a dance for him, some sort of rite?

Eurydice Which guidebook have you read?

Theseus I'd like to see it.
  Would you dance for me?

  Pause.

What's up? I'm asking you to dance with me

Eurydice You said for, dance for you

Theseus I said to dance

Eurydice I'm sorry but that isn't / what I heard

Theseus Don't apologise

Eurydice I'm not

Theseus No seriously, don't apologise
  In politics, you can't admit mistakes

Eurydice I haven't made one

Theseus You cannot be wrong

Eurydice I know that

Theseus So then. What are you afraid of? Dance.

  Neither moves.

  *First light. Miletus and Megaera sleep. Antigone is
  performing burial rites. She picks up a handful of dust.
  She lets it fall through her fingers over the corpse. She
  repeats the gesture. Junior Lieutenant Scud is watching
  her, curiously. Megaera wakes.*

Antigone I lead the blind
  I bury the dead
  I follow the path
  I am Antigone

  Megaera raises her gun. She aims it at Antigone.

Megaera Whoosh

Act Three

Tiresias enters with Harmonia. Ismene is making coffee –
a ceremony over charcoal.

Tiresias The ghosts
Their parched tongues are flickering
Like unseen negatives upon the day.
They form another city all round us

Ismene I'm not afraid of you, Tiresias.
You're like an old pet snake
Kept more out of pity than from fear

Harmonia holds out her hand. Ismene gives her a coin.

This child you've stolen from her mother
Any day now she'll be going to school.
You're irrelevant in our new Thebes

Tiresias The dead are not irrelevant. They're here

Theseus enters, with Phaeax and Talthybia. Eurydice
enters with her ministers.

Eurydice Good morning

Theseus Madam President

Eurydice You must try our Theban coffee

Theseus I did

Eurydice Shall we begin our conference?

Theseus There are people here who eat each other's
brains, people who believe that snakes can change your
gender. There are people who make roadblocks out of

63

human innards, people who leave corpses right outside their gates. Are you ready for a place at the table?

Eurydice How's your wife this morning? Have you managed to get hold of her?

Theseus My wife is not up for discussion here

He exits into the palace with Phaeax, Talthybia and retinue.

Euphrosyne What happened to him?

Eurydice Helia, Xenophanes and Bia
We'll start proceedings with your presentations

Xenophanes I don't think that's Theseus' plan

Helia Look at this agenda they've just given us
They've not scheduled any time for presentations

Bia Our plans are practical, beneficial, cheap
In five years we could be standing on our feet
If only he will listen

Eurydice We'll start as we intended
Agriculture, Education, Trade

Eris His men are armed, you know
Is that appropriate in there?

Eurydice They're bodyguards, not warlords

Eris There should be no weapons

Eurydice To take away their guns would frighten them
We don't want that

Xenophanes No more discussion.
Let's take the floor

They exit. Eurydice holds back Thalia, Euphrosyne and Aglaea. Eunomia also remains

Eurydice I have offended him

Thalia How?

Euphrosyne Child, whatever did you say?

Eurydice It isn't what I said
It isn't anything I did

Aglaea He made a pass at you

Eunomia I don't believe it

Thalia motions for Eunomia to stand further away..

Eurydice He said that he was offering equality

Aglaea The hound

Eurydice He said he envied me
He asked me what I was afraid of

Euphrosyne Oh gods, you turned him down

Thalia You have insulted him

Eurydice Maybe he was trying to make a link
To get beneath the mask
Perhaps I misinterpreted –
He didn't mean it as an insult –
Offered me an intimacy

Aglaea He just can't keep it zipped up in his suit

Thalia Don't be flippant

Aglaea This isn't flippancy

Thalia She has insulted the First Citizen of / Athens

Euphrosyne Gods
What can we do?
We must have his / goodwill

Thalia You can't pretend you didn't see it coming
You were flirting with him
All that stuff about the / seven heavens

65

Aglaea She had assumed equality, respect.
  She didn't realise these were gifts to be bestowed by him

Eurydice He'll mow me down in there
  He'll dance all over me
  The fate of Thebes hangs in the balance

Aglaea Thebes the beggar, yes;
  Not Thebes the whore.
  Well done
  You'll make a leader yet

Thalia Sister
  Words said in haste

Eurydice reaches for the senators.

Eurydice I think
  Under all the swagger
  He's incredibly alone
  And he can't communicate

Aglaea Are you seriously pitying him?

Euphrosyne If it was me
  I must confess
  I'd have that suit off in a minute
  The things you sacrifice for Thebes

Aglaea You get in there
  Exploit his weaknesses as he would exploit yours
  Now take a big deep breath

Eurydice and Aglaea are exiting into the palace.

Let's have some coffee in there, child

Thalia Our work is cut out now

Tydeus enters with Pargeia.

Eunomia What do you want here?

Pargeia We're coming to the conference
  So make way

Thalia Let me explain one more time
  You are the opposition

Tydeus So?

Eunomia Go away

  They exit.

Tydeus Opposition, yes
  Let's muster it
  The men want action

Pargeia Will you hold back?
  If we start an insurrection
  The Athenians will crush it.
  We need them on our side
  We have to get to Thesues

  Ismene has finished the coffee. She prepares to take it in.

Tydeus Look at this, Pargeia
  It's a real princess

Pargeia Forget that stuck-up little virgin

Tydeus That's no virgin
  It's an inbred royal

Ismene You're an embarrassment to Thebes

Pargeia Your own brother
  My dead husband lies unburied.
  This is the embarrassment to Thebes
  This is the barbarity
  And you, his sister, you do / nothing

Ismene Nothing, I do nothing, no

Pargeia *(to Tydeus)* Come here

We are getting in this conference
Now

Pargeia exits. Tydeus stares at Ismene.

Tydeus I like the way you keep our special secret.
I hear rape's a designated war crime now
And so I guess if you'd felt raped
You would have told.
Pleases me you treasure it.
You drew my blood
Kicking up against me in the dust.
Your teeth tore through my hand
You see that little scar?
My royal souvenir

Ismene Get back

Tydeus Bet there's no other man
Who makes your heartbeat race like that

Tydeus tries to touch her. Ismene pours the coffee on him.

Bitch
You're lucky all is peaceful now
You're lucky I'm so full of love

Pargeia (*re-entering*) Have I been talking to myself? I said get in

Tydeus Look at my fucking suit

Pargeia What did you do to him, you clumsy little slut? You keep away

Pargeia hits Ismene. Haemon enters.

You and your sister and your motherfucking dad

She spits, then exits with Tydeus.
Ismene tries to compose herself.

Haemon Antigone, where did you go?
Last night I woke and you were gone

Ismene No

Haemon Why did you run away?

Ismene / It's not –

Haemon Listen, let me say it, marry me
I love you more than anyone
You're passionate
And dazzling
And good and
All that grief
If it is loved
If you are loved
It won't hurt so unremittingly.
Please be my wife

Ismene exits. Tiresias is amused.

Haemon Antigone, Antigone

Tiresias Welcome to the country of the blind

*Megaera, Miletus and Scud enter with Antigone,
bound.*

Miletus (*to Haemon*) We need to see Eurydice

Haemon Who are you?

Megaera Her men

Miletus We have a prisoner for her

Haemon Who?

Megaera You can see for yourself

Haemon exits, without seeing Antigone.

Miletus They might reward us

Scud Who?

Miletus The ones who gave us all a vote

Scud I didn't vote

Miletus You're only old enough to kill, not vote

Antigone It's coming
My destiny
Swooping through the air
Atoms heavy with intention

Megaera Shut your face

Antigone The blow will hit me
Take me off my feet

Scud What blow?

Antigone I am ready

Scud What are atoms?

Miletus Don't be talking to her, Junior Lieutenant – she
is nuts

Scud She's right. There's something here

Megaera No, Scud

Scud (*raising his gun*) I can feel it: something bad

Megaera What are you, a dog?
You think you sense things humans can't?
Resist the madness, friend

Antigone You should have let me bury him

Megaera You shut your face

Scud It's like when those trees bent over us
The day my sister's spine was shot

Miletus Don't think of it, Lieutenant

Scud The trees bent forward / whispering

Miletus You were twisted up with drugs

Scud It was the shadow ones

Talthybia enters followed by Ismene.

Ismene I had the coffee made but then –

Talthybia crosses behind Scud dressed in grey. He spins round, sees her. He instantly has his gun trained on her.

Scud GHOST
GET DOWN
GHOST

Talthybia squirms on the floor. Ismene exits back into the palace.

Ismene EURYDICE

Miletus Don't shoot
/ Don't shoot

Ismene / EURYDICE

Scud DON'T MOVE

Megaera / That is not a shadow

The company enters from the palace.

Tydeus What the fuck / is this?

Miletus Scud, if you shoot her, we will be at war again

Scud / We are at war

Euphrosyne What's happening here?

Miletus At peace, Scud. / This is peace

Eris Thebans, put down your guns

Thalia / Oh gods
  Oh gods

  *Eurydice and Theseus enter, Phaeax behind them with
  Enyalius, Plautus and Ichnaea, armed.*

Enyalius Put down the gun or we will take you out

Eris / That is not the way

Megaera You take him out and I will kill this bitch down
dead

Enyalius Plautus – cover her

Eris / No guns
  No guns

Phaeax / Put the gun down, move away

  Megaera has her gun pointed at Antigone.

Plautus (*to Megaera*) One inch and I will kill you

Ismene Antigone
  / Antigone

Megaera I am fury

Antigone NO

Theseus What's happened here?

Enyalius Sir, please step back into the building

Miletus No one move

Enyalius Step back into the building, sir

Ichnaea Talthybia, you're fine

Eurydice What's happened here?

Theseus You need to get back in the building

Miletus We caught her burying the dead

Eurydice / Antigone

Talthybia I haven't buried / anyone

Scud Shut up
  / Shut up

Theseus Her name – quick

Ichnaea Talthybia

Theseus It's OK, Talthybia

Talthybia OK, OK

Scud Shut up you, stay there

Ismene Antigone, what have you done?

Eurydice is approaching Scud like a woman who has walked into gunfire before.

Eurydice No one here will harm you, soldier
  Please put down the gun

Theseus Now listen –

Miletus aims his gun at Theseus.

Miletus Don't move
  The Junior Lieutenant is my responsibility.
  NO ONE MOVE

Theseus is frozen.

Scud, look at me
  (*To Scud.*) She's not a ghost
  She is Athenian
  Touch her

Scud touches Talthybia. Eurydice slowly sits on the ground in front of him.

Scud We came to speak to someone

Eurydice I am someone. Speak to me

Scud Somebody who matters

Talthybia She is the –

Scud Shut your mouth, you bitch, or I will shoot

Eurydice I am Eurydice, your president.
There is no need for violence here
Let's all put down the guns

Miletus lowers his gun. Theseus' aides do not lower theirs – neither does Megaera.

Miletus OK, I'm lowering my gun
The Junior Lieutenant was mistaken, simply.
He means no one any harm

Theseus starts to breathe again.

Theseus I thought this palace was secure

Phaeax / These are palace guards, sir
They're supposed to be security

Eris You brought guns into a conference of peace

Theseus How close are we here to being terrorised and shot?

Eurydice This is one random action

Theseus So is the death of every president

Ichnaea Talthybia, stay down

Talthybia I'm fine, I'm cool, I'm desperately OK

Ichnaea (*to Miletus*) DON'T MOVE

Miletus Scud, tell them what we came for

Plautus changes position.

Megaera Don't move or I will kill her

Scud We were guarding someone. They were dead

Miletus Polynices

Scud As the dawn came I looked up.
Half the sky was shrouded in black cloud
The other half was blue and clear

Miletus You tell them why we're here

Scud That girl was digging, giving him the rites

Pargeia Antigone

Scud The earth was ready for him. Deep
Below me I could feel it gaping wide

Eurydice What is your name?

The Junior Lieutenant tries to remember it.

Miletus We call him Junior Lieutenant Scud

Eurydice The sky at dawn was trying to speak to you.
I know this because I saw it too.
It was telling us to choose our path.
We can choose the dark
Or chase the coming blue, the night cloud or the day.
Another life awaits you, my young son.
I hope it starts today
May blessings be upon you

Megaera lowers her gun.

(*To Scud.*) Now let your sergeant take the gun

Scud is reluctant.

Enyalius Sir, I need to get you back inside

Talthybia (*to Scud*) None of this is your responsibility
I can see that you are just a child

Scud, enraged by this, aims his gun at her again.

75

Scud I am not a child
I am a soldier

Phaeax fires. Scud falls against Talthybia, shot. Plautus
is disarming Megaera, Enyalius and Ichnaea; Miletus.
Megaera is thrown to the ground, Plautus' foot on her
back. Talthybia crying out in horror.

Miletus No, No –

Megaera SCUD

Plautus / On your face

Megaera SCUD

Plautus / I want you on your face

Miletus NO

Eurydice What have you done?

Talthybia cries out.

Ichnaea / It's OK
Talthybia, it's cool

Pargeia Get in there. Pick him up –

Haemon (*to Ismene*) Take me to him

Pargeia I said pick him up

Tydeus does so.

Theseus He was about to kill one of my staff

Thalia Oh gods / Oh gods

Aglaea Disaster /
Disaster

Tydeus I've got you, soldier

Theseus Who is in charge?

Miletus I got him through the war
  Right through the war
  I saw him through it to the end
  And now you cunts –

Phaeax We did our job
  / We did what's right

Enyalius / Shut up

Miletus You've no idea
  No fucking clue

Plautus Don't move

Theseus Who controls this rabble?

Eurydice I'm responsible

Theseus Where is your chief of staff?

Eurydice I haven't yet appointed one

Tydeus It should be me, Prince Tydeus

Aglaea Never

Tydeus You can't have a military force without a leader
  / This is the result

Eurydice I am the leader

Megaera You stand and let them disarm Theban men?
You bitch of Athens

Pargeia That's right, sister, speak your mind

Megaera / I'll shout it from the walls what you have
done

Eurydice Will you call your men away?

*Theseus gestures. His men lower their guns. Scud is
dying.*

Haemon Who has first aid? One of you Athenians must have first aid

Phaeax I'm trained
I have first aid

Haemon THEN MOVE
How can you watch me and not help?
HE'S DYING

Phaeax and Ichnaea go to assist.

Megaera SCUD
/ SCUD

Thalia The war is over. Why is this boy still in a uniform?

Miletus There's nothing else for him but begging

Megaera SCUD

Miletus They made a killer of him overnight
Do you expect he'll just as easily become a boy again?

Tydeus Weak Theban leadership has almost killed King Theseus

Euphrosyne You damned hyena
Here to feast upon a dead boy's corpse

Tydeus You almost sent the hope of Athens
Home to his good people in a box
/ This is how incapable these women are

Thalia Theseus, this is a war criminal
/ He means destruction I can promise you

Tydeus Who knows the situation with these armed militias? Me
Who can control them? Me
Who do you need here?

Pargeia Prince Tydeus

Haemon Get him in
  ALL OF YOU GET HIM INSIDE
  I need clean water
  Bright dazzling lights
  Ismene

Ismene Here

Haemon Help me

Thalia Take him in there. Get him on the table

  They exit, Miletus, Megaera and Thalia with them.

Aglaea (*to Euphrosyne*) We're going to the barracks,
now.
  We need the remnants of the army on our side

Euphrosyne / I am with you

  They exit.

Pargeia (*to Tydeus*) Go to your men; prepare them.

Tydeus His blood is –

Pargeia Give me some

Tydeus Piglets

Pargeia I'll say I held him by your side

Tydeus Mama would never pay the butcher for the task
  We'd hang them up and slit their piggy throats

Pargeia Forget the pigs

Tydeus Catching all the splatter in a pail

Pargeia Tell Theseus you love him. Now

Tydeus I am at your service, Theseus

  All go except Eurydice, Theseus and Antigone.
  The Bodyguards also remain, on high alert.

Harmonia has watched the death of Scud with horror.
She is riveted by all that follows.

Eurydice You sanctioned murder in my house

Theseus I think you'll find that I contained an incident

Eurydice Who rules this land now, Theseus?

Theseus It's ruled by every wild card with a gun who walks in through your gates. My mandate's to / protect my people

Eurydice Your mandate's to provide peacekeepers, not to start another war

Theseus Who was aggressor there?

Eurydice The men who shot that boy

Theseus They kept the peace

Eurydice I had the peace. I had it in my hand. He was about to / give away his gun

Theseus To kill my citizen

Antigone I'm fighting with the gods of death
    They are above ground
    I'm trying to appease
    To do what they require

Theseus She was burying her brother
    Who would not?

Antigone I've fought with them and begged
    And now
    They're feeding on that boy.
    This is not
    Is not my destiny

Talthybia enters. She is covered in blood.

Talthybia He's dead. Your son tried what he could but –

Eurydice Thank you very much, Talthybia

Talthybia The table
He is lying on the table
Blood
The documents are
All his blood

Tiresias The sun will not race through the day
Before you have surrendered up
One born of your own loins
To feed the gods of death, for what you've done

Theseus What is it with that hag?

Eurydice Tiresias

Theseus Why do you tolerate her here?
How can a modern state have room for this?
(*To Tiresias.*) Who were you speaking to? To her
Or me? Whose loins?
What the fuck are loins supposed to be?
Do men and women both have loins –
Well do they?

Talthybia I don't know, sir

Theseus What do you have, hag?

Tiresias The day comes soon when grief
Will break like waves through halls of power.
A suicide and then a son

Theseus Whose son? What suicide?

Tiresias It's coming. It will come

Antigone Many years ago when Oedipus was young
Tiresias saved Thebes. There was an epidemic
And his revelations saved us. He said

My father was the curse upon our land.
Oedipus was murderous incestuous corruption
And his children, all of us so small
He called a crowd of horrors

Eurydice Antigone

Theseus What else has she foreseen?

Eurydice I never listen to a word

Theseus What has it said?

Eurydice Tiresias has only ever spoken once to me. It was
just before you came
　I took it as a joke. He said

Tiresias 'If you intend to fuck the god of power, don't
fall asleep beside him'

Theseus And do you?

Eurydice Do I what?

Theseus Intend to fuck with him?

Eurydice I don't see him anywhere

Theseus Miss

Talthybia My name's / Talthybia

Theseus Could you please organise an imminent
departure?

Eurydice DON'T

Theseus Since I stepped on Theban soil I've felt unclean;
as if your vile, atavistic war was all my goddam fault. /
How dare you –

Eurydice Are we not behaving like the pets you hoped
to tame?
　Are you discovering instead of women pliable and
biddable

That we're passionate and human; that we're free?
No one wants a strong and healthy Thebes, not you,
not Sparta

Theseus From now on you will be dealing with my
people. My sense of international responsibility, my
goddam decency prevents me pulling out my men today

Eurydice You're going to run away?

Theseus My personal involvement with you ends right
now

Eurydice That is not leadership

Theseus My life was put in danger here. I could have
died

Eurydice DON'T GO

Theseus You have / not said a single word

Eurydice Do not abandon us

Theseus There has been no apology

Eurydice I'm begging you
  I'm sorry
  Please don't go

Theseus Pathetic

> *Theseus exits. Phaeax enters, also covered in blood.
> He is doing his best to clean his hands with surgical
> wipes*

Phaeax Where's Theseus? We need to know what his
instructions are for the disposal of the body

Eurydice THAT IS THEBAN BUSINESS

Talthybia Theseus has just informed us that his diplomatic
mission here is over

Phaeax Oh

Talthybia Have you got anything to say?

Phaeax I have some wipes here
  You should use them
  You should really clean yourself
  The blood you know
  It might be –
  Look
  I've only got first aid
  I'm not a surgeon
  And that Theban guy
  He couldn't see
  I saved your life
  You were down there in the dust
  That psycho had a gun right at your head
  I was aiming for his arm, OK? (*He approaches her.*)
  You know I'm not at liberty to take responsibility for this
  If I accept responsibility then our insurance policy won't cover me
  There is a protocol I have to follow here, you know that.
  But off the record, strictly off the record
  Sorry

Talthybia You are going to be my bitch
  You understand that?
  You are now my bitch

  Talthybia exits.

Phaeax Fuck

  Phaeax exits. Harmonia inches forward.

Eurydice So this is not your destiny?

  Antigone shakes her head.

I can't believe

That you would side
With Prince Tydeus and the tyrant's wife
I thought that your integrity was absolute
So pure you make the rest of us feel tainted

Antigone For me alone
I had to bury him

Eurydice Why?

Antigone Because it's right

Eurydice Out of your rightness what will come?
A boy is dead
The citizen of Athens turns his back
I should throw you in a stinking cell for this
What do you think will happen?

Antigone Send me to the dark

Eurydice So Prince Tydeus can take up your part?
That widowed spider's spinning up support;
The forces I have tried so hard to quell
Are baying once again for power
This is the entry into chaos

Antigone Let me
In the dark and squalor of a cell
Give me the means
I'll kill myself
To die is to be free

Eurydice Antigone

Antigone I'm no different from my brother
I have a violent, prehistoric heart
I should be dead with Polynices
Let me be dead

Eurydice I could have smothered him in flesh-dissolving
lime

And dumped him in the ground
But
What he did to Creon, to Menoceus my boy –
What he did to Thebes
I hated him
I hate him
My heart is violent and it's vengeful too
And I have dressed it up as reparation
Shrouded it in reconciliation
Saying maybe we will learn from staring at his face
The face of chaos. Maybe we'll choose life,
Life and order and society
As the alternative is him. But when
I stared down at the mottled thing
I felt euphoria of savage hate
It made me glad to see him rot.
It is an act of hatred that I've done
A desecration
And I'm guilty
And it is my fault
I caused that child soldier's death
And lost the help of Athens.
This is the match that lights my own destruction
Not to do what I've exhorted all my countrymen to do:
Be reconciled.
I cannot reconcile
I hate him, still I hate
He took my boy and mutilated him
And if I'm full of vicious, unforgiving hate
The moderate and principled
New president of Thebes
What future is there for us?

Antigone Ismene thinks about the future all the time and
Haemon too.
    I've never understood their lack of fear.
    My future's always been the desolate track

86

I walked on with my father
Leading on ahead past rotting crops and bloated dogs
Through burning villages, through war.
Oedipus was saved the sight
But I saw my destiny, my destination
Death

Eurydice Oedipus
The way he fed upon your spirit
Took the youth in you and made it old
Dragged your hand through all his suffering
He was a selfish, blind old man

*Harmonia looks from Antigone to Tiresias. Tiresias
requires a drink. She serves him.*

My son Haemon is in love with you
I wish it was Ismene but it's you
You know that, don't you?

Antigone Yes

Eurydice You see the antidote to suffering
The opposite of great heroic destiny
Is a quiet ordinary life: to love.
You've done enough for death, Antigone
You can retire from service I would say
Tiresias please tell her she is free

Tiresias I only see a suicide
A woman hanging by the neck
Her hair like trailing moss

Eurydice You are despicable

Tiresias I wish I could see differently
The shadow of that boy
He's watching you

This deeply unsettles Harmonia.

Antigone What's to be done?

Eurydice There's no such thing as destiny
There's only change

Antigone Please will you bury my brother?

Eurydice You're asking me to admit my mistake

Antigone You already have

Eurydice In politics, I'll die

Antigone I never see the politics
I'm blind to them

Eurydice No, you see too clearly;
You've always seen through me
Right through my careful mask.
If I am weak
If I turn round and put that carcass in the earth
I fear the enemies of freedom
Will run me down like painted wolves.

The soldiers, Haemon, Ismene and the senators enter.
They are carrying the dead Junior Lieutenant.
Harmonia picks up Tiresias' staff. She sings, high and
free. A funeral song.

Harmonia
The gods of death
Have feasted here

Lift your soul
Up to Elysium

May you be free
May you be free

The procession passes. Harmonia, Eurydice and
Antigone become a part of it. Tiresias remains.

Act Four

Two graves. The senators between them, Antigone,
Haemon, Ismene, Miletus, Megaera; bystanders,
Polykleitos among them. Eurydice stares at both graves,
covered with the mud of digging.

Haemon The crowd, Mumma
    They need to hear you speak

Eurydice is silent, head bowed.

Talk to the crowd

Eurydice This heavy mask of power.
    It will tear off my face

Haemon When they pulled the shrapnel from my eyes.
    And I was lying, knowing that my useful life was over
    You washed me, dressed me and you said get up.
    I'd have liked it if you'd rained down tears
    But you handed me a stick. Get up

Haemon helps her up. She turns to the crowd.

Thalia Your strongest words

Eurydice By insulting Polynices
    I've insulted all the dead.
    I have been wrong
    I'm trying to turn back time one hour
    And it keeps buckling against me, flying on
    The death of Junior Lieutenant Scud
    Is my responsibility
    I won't insult him with my sorrow and my shame
    But I must give his death some value

Since his life was held so cheap.
Today, we've buried two dead Theban boys;
One, in life a mighty powerful man
One still a child, without a proper name.
General Polynices, son of Oedipus
And Junior Lieutenant Scud.
The way we treat these boys in death
Must illuminate how we intend to live
The Junior Lieutenant will be honoured,
Foremost son of Thebes.
Polynices will lie at his feet,
Marked only with his name.
In death, the general will wait upon the child

Thalia In death, the general will wait upon the child

Polykleitos kneels. Thalia kneels. The rest follow suit.

ELSEWHERE: *Tydeus and Pargeia.*

Tydeus My arteries are coursing with my god
My Dionysus, my amphetamine

Pargeia Where are our men?

Tydeus They're plucked up from the gutters, shacks and bars
Shaken, made alive with guns.
I've been up there on my truck
With Spartan weapons in my hand
Preaching revolution, Theban style.
The coup, swift and irrevocable
Has always favoured men like me –

Pargeia Stop now
Hold back
You keep them on the leash

Tydeus The open tear in time won't last
I feel it closing even now –

Pargeia Eurydice has left the web.
    The big presidential spider
    Should be in the centre
    Feeling every shift upon the net
    But she's gone, she's scuttled off
    Theseus is all alone up here
    And enmity's between him and Eurydice

Tydeus I have to do some politics

Pargeia Shape up to it, come on, shape up
    Shine up that skilful tongue of yours
    We could have Theseus without the violence.
    If Athens backs us Thebes is ours – elections all be
fucked
    You know it's Athens chooses leaders, props them up.
    All this blah-blah-blah about democracy –
    If they don't like the people's choice, they topple it

Tydeus Why do you always have the fucking plan?

    He tries to kiss her.

Pargeia No time for that
    Not yet, my Prince
    But soon

    She gives him a promise of something more.

Don't go in to Theseus all painted like a wolf.
    That gives the wrong impression straight away

Tydeus I'm going for gold, Pargeia

Pargeia Go for gold

    ELSEWHERE: *by the graves.*

    Euphrosyne and Aglaea speak intimately with Eurydice.

Aglaea Tydeus has coiled up his men
    And they are waiting
    Stationed round the palace set to spring

Euphrosyne We have secured the military with promises of money we don't have. The remnants of the factions – they will fight for you

Eurydice It must not come to that
Our mission must remain a peaceful one
Or what have we become?

Euphrosyne Our government's unique in all the world. It is worth fighting for

Eurydice Our government will be unique if we can maintain power without resort to violence. That is the thing worth fighting for

Aglaea I have imposed a no-fly zone.
Under the circumstances it seemed pertinent.
It also means that Theseus can't leave

Eurydice You genius

Aglaea You must get back.
To spend hours kneeling in the sun
It is not wise

Eurydice It is essential

Pargeia enters.

Pargeia Thebes, you do not have a president, you have a coward
First she desecrates my husband's corpse
And then, when she perceives the horror of her crime
She quickly throws my Polynices in the ground

Antigone Did your husband bury those he slew?

Eurydice Antigone

Antigone Their bodies rot there still in fields and streets.
And now he's dead you've got the next best thing
Apprentice tyrant Prince Tydeus

Pargeia Tydeus is the leader that we need
  He does the work of gods

Antigone I saw his work in villages
  Women, little girls
  All dead and stinking
  Seething with the ants

  *Megaera cocks her gun at Antigone – an automatic
  gesture of defence.*

Pargeia You have no shred of evidence against the Prince

Ismene I do

  Megaera stands with Pargeia. She lowers her gun.

Pargeia Thebans, Theseus is leaving
  Eurydice has driven him away.
  He is packing up
  And with him goes our hope.
  Who wants their children to be fed?
  Who wants a future of prosperity?
  March with me to the palace
  Where your Prince is now with Theseus
  Prince Tydeus, trying to mend
  What these incompetents have broken.
  He is now our hope –
  The Prince
  Come with me for the Prince

Megaera The Prince

Pargeia The Prince

  *Pargeia exits. Megaera follows with some of the crowd.
  Cries of 'The Prince'.*

Eurydice I wish that Thebes could mend itself without
the rich world's help. I wish that we could find the unity,
the strength. But in the meantime invite the Spartans to
the talks

Aglaea Thank you
　　I must confess
　　I did already
　　They arrive tonight
　　Say nothing; sack me later

Eurydice You should be our leader

Aglaea Yes, but no one likes me. They elected you

Eurydice Citizens of Thebes
　　Theseus is not about to leave
　　We will secure his friendship – that I promise you.
　　In less than one hour's time
　　We will have the hand of Athens in our own
　　And all our future hopes secure

　　She turns to go.

Aglaea Can we deliver that?

Eurydice Now I've said it, we will have to

　　Eurydice exits with her senators.

Thalia You said 'I do'
　　Evidence
　　Tydeus
　　What do you have?

Ismene Nothing
　　I have nothing, no

Thalia Please find your courage
　　Speak

Ismene No evidence
　　I scrubbed it all away

Antigone Ismene

Ismene I'm going to Athens. I'll ask Theseus to let me tag along: a souvenir of Thebes. In Athens I wouldn't

94

have to be a relic from this house. I could wear jeans and smoke

Antigone How can you be flippant?

Ismene I think it's in my nature, buried under years, to be quite shallow and to laugh. I think alone of Oedipus' children I've got a sense of humour. Burying our brother nearly split my sides. And the biggest joke of all is that Haemon has proposed. He has asked you, Antigone, to be his wife.
  It was a nice proposal; very sweet.
  But by mistake
  The stupid, eyeless oaf made it to me.
  (*To Haemon.*) I've been in love with you since I was nine

  Ismene exits.

Antigone Ismene
  ISMENE

  Antigone runs off after her.

Thalia Polykleitos. You could tell them what Tydeus did

Polykleitos I don't think I could get my mouth to move

Thalia What if he becomes respectable?
  That's what he intends
  Come with me

Polykleitos Who'd believe? The people who can shout with passion always win. There is no point

Haemon They win because the men like you, the best of us, keep quiet

Miletus What happened to your eyes?

Haemon I'm blind
  I couldn't save your friend

Miletus Early in the war
The general I was with
Would kill a child before each fight
And we would drink the blood.
The place I was
Was so far gone
That I could see no harm.
One night I woke to find a bushknife at my neck
A woman holding it
Her hands were stinking with our blood
I was the only soldier she had left alive
'You are our sons,' she said
And somewhere in me
What was human in me woke.
She said she'd spare my life and lift her curse
If I could save as many as I'd killed.
I managed only two
Just one remains.

*Harmonia sings. Miletus leaves his gun on Scud's
grave. He exits.*
Harmonia gives Haemon Tiresias' staff.
Antigone enters.

Antigone Ismene said, 'Can you not see?'

Haemon Antigone

Antigone I want to see
What life is like
To live

Act Five

Theseus and Tydeus enter.

Tydeus The women turn him on
  They get him all worked up with dancing
  Then they run off to the mountains
  To perform their rites.
  And Pentheus can't find
  The thing, you know
  The thing that makes us men

  Talthybia enters.

Theseus He loses his –

Tydeus Not quite physically –
  All the inside stuff

Theseus Testosterone?

Tydeus Not quite

Talthybia Excuse me
  This is Prince Tydeus

Theseus Yes, I know that

Talthybia He's accused of war crimes, Theseus

Theseus I think I left the phone you gave me in my quarters. Would you go and see if there's a message from my son?

  Talthybia exits.

So Pentheus is unmanned

Tydeus With the help of Dionysus he applies some make-up and he dresses up

Theseus He wants to find out what it's like to be a woman?

Tydeus Have you never wondered, sir?
  The myths are where we risk
  What we would never think in life.
  Pentheus was mad with longing
  He was desperate to join the rites

Theseus To dance

Tydeus He follows them into the wild
  He climbs a tree
  He watches all their secrets
  Feels as isolated as a star
  He cries
  His tears go splash upon the women underneath
  They look up.
  Red alert
  A man in drag

Theseus What do they do?

Tydeus I can't believe you come to Thebes and you don't know this story. That great gang of naked women dragged Pentheus on to the ground and pulled him limb from limb with their bare hands. Those ladies and those little girls dismembered him. They tore his dick off and his head off and his own mother and his aunts were playing with his body parts like they were bits of ram goat ready for the grill

Theseus Shit

The sound of a crowd begins to approach.

Tydeus That's quite a story, isn't it?

Theseus That's fucking elemental

Tydeus It's true
(*Pointing to Tiresias.*) You ask her
She was there

Tiresias The furies
Zeus himself bows down to them
One of them is coming
An avenger to destroy you

Theseus Oh shut up
Shut up
I'm going to build a care home here
For beggarly transgender types
I'm going to take you off the street
Stick you on a rocking chair in front of a TV
And feed you the strongest psychotropic drugs
That medicine can buy

Tiresias Where is my child?
I bought her from her mother
She is mine

Tydeus You can see why we're all wary of the womenfolk
round here

Phaeax enters.

Phaeax Sir, we've just been told that Thebes is in a state
of high alert. Crowds are marching through the streets.
A no-fly zone has been imposed

Theseus Excuse me?

Phaeax Air space has been / prohibited

Theseus I know what a no-fly zone is

Phaeax The Theban senators insist we stay in our
chambers until such time as they can guarantee our safety

Theseus Are you a moron?

Phaeax No, sir

Theseus Yes, I think you are

Phaeax This information you may judge to be moronic. I am merely its deliverer

Theseus You pulled your trigger on that boy. You were his deliverer. It was moronic

Talthybia enters.

Phaeax We were aiming to disarm, not kill.
We followed your own protocol
I protected you
And then I tried to save his life.
I don't know why I'm getting all this shit

Talthybia (*handing Theseus the mobile*) Theseus, you have no messages

Theseus hands the mobile to Phaeax.

Theseus Get me my son, Hippolytus. I want to talk to him right now. He's stationed up at Troezen under General Pirithous. Young man –

Phaeax Yes, sir?

Theseus Don't cry in front of me

Phaeax exits.

Theseus Tell Eurydice that I have no intention of resuming talks

Talthybia Sir, if I may –

Theseus Her no-fly zone is a pathetic ruse to keep me here

Talthybia There's a crowd approaching, some / sort of protest –

Theseus Get it lifted, crowd or not

Talthybia exits.

Those women ripping up King Pentheus –
   That's just a myth, that's not your history, right?

Tydeus All violence in Thebes is mythic
   It soon fades into the past
   Loses its immediacy and force.
   You'll find our civil war is mythic too
   Blown into distorted shapes.
   The violence happened
   But it wasn't real

Theseus That's a disturbing answer

Tydeus I can keep order here in Thebes
   I'd see your will was done.
   I'd make sure that Thebes becomes whatever you desire
   Thebes needs a man like you;
   You're strong and clear; you give us hope
   And in this small, material world
   First Citizen of Athens
   You're the nearest thing to Dionysus that I've ever seen

Phaeax enters. The sound of the crowd is much nearer.

Phaeax Sir, I spoke with General Pirithous. He says your
son Hippolytus is absent without leave. He left the base
last night to see your wife, at your request. Since then,
nothing has been heard of him. The general is offering to
search your coastal residence

Theseus Thank him. Tell him yes

Phaeax There is a crowd sir, gathering down there. The
peacekeepers await your orders. What should I be telling
them?

Theseus To keep the peace

Phaeax And how should they interpret that?

Theseus Could you get out of here?

Phaeax exits.

I'm strangely –
  Since I got here I have –
  My conviction, yes, my certainty has gone.
  My easy access to the gods themselves:
  Suddenly it's all obscured.
  I feel some revelation, some disaster is at hand

Tydeus Theseus

Theseus Said way too much. I'm going to walk away

Tydeus It's Thebes that is off-centre, not yourself.
  You stick an upright man into a gale,
  A cyclone, and the cyclone will prevail.
  Thebes hasn't done with chaos yet.

*Pargeia enters. Megaera stays by the door. She watches
Prince Tydeus closely.*

Eurydice will never hold it back
  The very female nature is chaotic.
  They can't structure or impose
  They won't inspire respect
  The woman
  She should do what she was made for

Pargeia And what's that?

Tydeus Pargeia

Pargeia I've led the people up to greet you, Theseus
  They would so appreciate a glimpse

Theseus For what?

Pargeia News has been leaked that you are going to leave
us. Violence is erupting. People feel Eurydice has let them

down; they feel betrayed. They've come to beg you not to go. I know you haven't taken well to Thebes but we could find a lot of ways to make your visits here a pleasure

Eurydice enters with Aglaea and Euphrosyne. She is still covered in dirt from digging.

Eurydice Theseus
You are free to leave at any time.
We will ensure safe passage through our air space

Theseus Have you still got authority?

Eurydice Thank you for everything you've done here
It has been a pleasure speaking with you – genuinely.
Now if you'll excuse us, we've a conference to prepare
We expect the Spartans shortly

Theseus What?

Euphrosyne The Spartans are arriving

Eurydice I was hoping beggars could be choosers but it seems we can't

Theseus Let me tell you about Sparta

Euphrosyne We are not ignorant

Theseus The Spartans do not tolerate the weak

Aglaea We are not weak

Theseus They feel no responsibility to improve your lot. They're here to feast upon your natural resources. You can be sure of that

Aglaea And Athens offers us an economic zone

Theseus They'll strip you bare

Eurydice Our people go to bed with hunger craving in their bellies every night. Right now we'll entertain any regime that gives us means to feed them

Theseus If you want an independent, democratic Thebes –

Eurydice I want people to survive
Mine are the politics of dire need.
I am president of famine
First citizen of rubble, plague and debt
And hungry dogs are scavenging the waste.
Athens, Sparta
If you cannot help
May you devour yourselves

Theseus I can't believe you'd speak to me like this.
I came here so compassionate
So full of energy, of admiration;
I was going to pledge myself to your improvement.
You make me feel like I'm a wicked man
And I don't like that, not one bit.
I AM THE HOPE OF ATHENS AND THE WORLD

Eurydice Then come out with me and tell the crowd

Pause.

Tydeus How can I assist you, Theseus?
Because to bring the Spartans into things
That is an insult
I'm insulted here on your behalf

Pargeia After everything you've done for Thebes

Tydeus I would never deal with the Spartans

Euphrosyne Unless you're buying weapons from them

Tydeus You know what I'm reminded of?
With all these ladies situated here
Hyenas trying their weight against the lions

Talthybia enters with Thalia and Polykleitos.

Theseus Tabitha, I asked my aide to make a call for me –

Talthybia My name's Talthybia
Please have the courtesy to get it right.
This is Polykleitos, a mechanic
And you know the Minister of Justice, Thalia

Thalia Please will you witness this man's testimony?

Polykleitos You were my hero
I taught my son to love you
We had you on a poster
Your face
Tacked up on our garage wall.
I've meditated on your face
That tsetse face

Tydeus I don't know you, brother

Polykleitos We were hiding from the massacre
My son was terrified.
His name was Opheltes and he was five years old
You shot the locks
We saw you kick the door
The light surrounded you
That grin.
My son, he ran to you
As if you were a hero come to save us.
And
You pinned him on a bayonet
You lifted him
Laughed at your strength as you held him aloft
Shaking the gun
The blood dropped like rain
My boy
Bewildered at his death.
Your twisting laugh;
It rings in my ears in the night

Tydeus I don't know you

Polykleitos You killed my son
You burned my home
You don't know me
I am the coward who hid
And watched the flames
Even as they
Even as they ate

Tydeus I'm so sorry for your loss
But you're mistaken, friend

Polykleitos I know the moment lies in wait for you
When Opheltes in all his blood-dimmed innocence
Will step into your mind and shake your sanity to pieces

Megaera Whoosh

Polykleitos I'd like to go

Polykleitos exits with Thalia. The noise of the restless crowd is louder.

Eurydice Excuse me
The future will not wait

Aglaea Thank you for your interest in Thebes

Eurydice exits with Aglaea and Euphrosyne.

Pargeia Theseus, if you would step outside with Prince Tydeus and myself, I think that we could calm the situation down

Theseus You must be so naive
Political babies, both of you.
You are untouchable;
A tyrant's wife, a warlord

Tydeus But privately, when you and I were speaking –

Theseus I don't recall I ever met you
This private conversation is a myth

Tydeus Our paths will cross again
　　Much sooner than you think
　　And when they do
　　We will remember this

　　Tydeus and Pargeia leave. Megaera follows them.

Theseus I'm cold
　　I felt a sudden fear go down my back
　　My hairs are standing up

Talthybia Thebes has a very strong effect.
　　I'd like to stay here
　　The Theban attitude would seem to be
　　That in the face of our destruction
　　The only thing humanity can do
　　Is to create

　　Phaeax enters.

Phaeax Sir, I've General Pirithous on the phone

Theseus What is it?

Phaeax He
　　Is at your home

Theseus What is it?

　　ELSEWHERE: *Pargeia, Tydeus, Megaera enter.*

Pargeia You fucked it up
　　You fucked it up

Tydeus You fat degenerate obscene salacious slut

Pargeia I am not fat

Tydeus You fucking threw yourself at him

Pargeia You were in love with him
　　I saw it in your eyes

Big Theseus
You dumb cocksucker

Tydeus I had him so he almost called me brother

Pargeia You would have given him your naked butt
If I had not arrived.
You're all the same, you men
You go round raping women to disguise the fact
You like it from each other best

Tydeus You're filth

Pargeia I'm debris, I am waste, I'm dereliction, I am
frenzy

Tydeus You could survive in hell itself

Pargeia I have.
Give your men the word

Tydeus It's time

Pargeia Unleash the god of uproar on this town

Tydeus Uproar

Pargeia Cry fury

Tydeus / Fury

Megaera Fury

Megaera stabs Tydeus. He falls against Pargeia.

Pargeia What have you done?

Megaera I have seen that mouth before
Against the sun, above me, twisting, hurting
In a village by a river where I used to be a girl

Pargeia Prince –

Megaera Let me go now, furies
Let me go

Megaera exits.

Eurydice is washing. Ismene waiting.

Eurydice I can go out without him
Go out before the people quite alone.
I'll tell them Thebes must find a way
To be a nation that regenerates itself
That without the crumbs of help
From monstrous foreign powers
We can begin to grow

Ismene That is a fantasy
I'm sorry but your optimism's ludicrous
It sickens me

Eurydice Ismene –

Ismene What special quality allows you to believe
That you can challenge or change anything?

Eurydice What's happened?
My sweet girl

Ismene Not sweet
Not girl
Forgive me
I have not survived this war

   Theseus enters.

Theseus You refuse to see me

Eurydice This is my private room

Theseus That is childish
And it is a great mistake

Eurydice I have not refused to see you – I am washing

Theseus I offered you equality

Eurydice No you did not

Theseus It's not equality you want

You think yourself superior in every way
Behaving like a prehistoric queen

Eurydice Theseus, I am a beggar not a queen
I beg you to keep faith with me
And with my government.
Come before the people with me please
Or everything I'm fighting for is lost.
I have no desire to sell myself to Sparta
If it comes to that then I would rather dance for you

Pause.

Theseus Two snakes, slithering mistrust
That's what your prophet said.
Do you think in essence
That it's like that with a woman and a man?

Eurydice If they're politicians.
I would love to trust you, Theseus

Theseus I got a call
From General Pirithous
He is in my house
He said –

Eurydice What is it?

Theseus Phaedra
She is dead

Theseus is suddenly exhausted, as if a great shock has hit him.

Eurydice Ismene

Ismene gets a stool.

Theseus Phaedra
She is hanging
Hanging from the beam
Above our bed.

Theseus half collapses. She helps him onto the stool.

The scale of chaos here:
    To mend it is beyond me.
    The haemorrhage of cash
    The manpower it would need
    To bring Thebes to prosperity –

Eurydice Theseus

Theseus I knew
    That something in my life was going to break
    Phaedra
    My son

Eurydice Where is he?

Theseus They don't know
    What did he do to her?
    He hated her

Eurydice You cannot know that it was him

Theseus Curse him

Eurydice Please don't say that

Theseus CURSE HIM

Eurydice You are speaking in your grief

Theseus I know your government is brave
    And you deserve success.
    Forgive me but –
    I haven't got the –
    Cannot deal with Sparta
    But
    I'll come outside with you
    Give you my hand

Eurydice I married Creon at sixteen
    He was forty-five.
    The young feel such despair

Phaedra
There was a time –
To die like that
It could have been my end

Theseus I'm sorry that I asked you for a dance

Eurydice These fists of yours
One force, one gentleness
Open them

Theseus Athens
Come to Athens
We will reconvene
You have my word

Eurydice Next time we meet
I hope that when our battle's done
We'll see each other
Masks off, as ourselves

Theseus Eurydice
Perhaps we'll risk our trust

They exit, out to the crowd.

ELSEWHERE: *Antigone enters with Haemon. She sees
Tiresias, alone. She helps him up.*

Antigone What do you see, Tiresias?

Tiresias My child has gone

Antigone Where is my destiny?

Tiresias In darkness

Antigone You see nothing?

Tiresias Nothing, no

Antigone Then the future's mine to make

Haemon The future is the country of the blind. It must
belong to me

Antigone In Athens, they have great machines that see inside your head. In Athens, they have doctors who could mend your eyes

Haemon Not just mend; they can transplant. They take the eyes from fresh cadavers and with surgery as skilful and as delicate as art, they can insert them in a blind man's skull. In Athens we could see through reawakened eyes. What do you say to that, Tiresias?

Antigone I say it is a land of miracles

Tiresias Numberless indignant birds
Are making storm clouds in Athenian skies.
One day men of Thebes, as conquerors
Will walk into that devastated town
And sweep away the ruins of its power.
Greed that eats, will eat itself.
Athens' time will come

Aides prepare for a departure, taking all the paraphernalia of a diplomatic visit.

Polykleitos continues his work.

The senators enter, preparing for the arrival of the Spartans.

Through the politics, Antigone, leading the blind men.

Ismene, dressed in Athenian clothes, pleads with Phaeax to be let on the helicopter. He is unforthcoming. She exits after him, still pleading.

Talthybia enters. Tiresias' child is holding papers for her. They crouch together in the blast. Talthybia loses her hair-do. They exit, as the noise of the helicopter begins to fade.

Epilogue

Dust and emptiness – but for the figure of Miletus.
  Megaera enters.

Megaera Miletus, where are you going?

Miletus Athens

Megaera Why?

Miletus Because I want

Megaera Want what?

Miletus That stuff they got

Megaera And what's that?

Miletus Everything

Megaera But Athens
  They won't let us in

Miletus You coming too?

Megaera I'll keep you company
  As long as you don't give me all your shit

Miletus Be fair

Megaera That sergeant shit
  Don't try and pull that
  You are not my sergeant now

Miletus I'm just the man that's standing here
  His pockets full of breeze.
  There's nothing more to me than this

Megaera That's man enough for me

Miletus Glad to hear it
Glad you finally have eyes

Megaera So how you going to get to Athens, in your limousine?

Miletus The Theban way

Megaera How's that?

Miletus On my big Theban feet

Megaera It's far away

Miletus So far away they got a different sky

Megaera They don't like Thebans there

Miletus I heard that too

Megaera We're likely to get shut outside their gates

Miletus That's right. At best, they'll give us shitty jobs like sweeping up their streets

Megaera Their streets are clean already. And those dingy places no one wants to live, I hear they've all got flushing toilets and TVs

Miletus Athens has a lot of crime

Megaera That's right. It's quite a violent place

Miletus You think you'll handle it?

Megaera I cannot wait. You think they'll stop us at the gates?

Miletus Megaera, woman, what do you suggest?

Megaera Miletus, man,
They give us any shit
They stand there in their marble palaces and try to keep us out
We'll soak our rags in petrol
And we'll burn their city down